THE POMERANIAN

Lexiann Grant

The Pomeranian

Project Team
Editor: Cynthia P. Gallagher
Copy Editor: Ann Fusz
Design: Angela Stanford
Series Design: Mada Design and Stephanie Krautheim
Series Originator: Dominique De Vito

T.F.H. Publications
President/CEO: Glen S. Axelrod
Executive Vice President: Mark E. Johnson
Publisher: Christopher T. Reggio
Production Manager: Kathy Bontz

T.F.H. Publications, Inc.
One TFH Plaza
Third and Union Avenues
Neptune City, NJ 07753

06 07 08 09 10 1 3 5 7 9 8 6 4 2
Printed and bound in China
Library of Congress Cataloging-in-Publication Data
Grant, Lexiann.
  The Pomeranian / Lexiann Grant.
     p. cm.
  Includes index.
  ISBN 0-7938-3646-8 (alk. paper)
  1. Pomeranian dog. I. Title.
  SF429.P8G73 2006
  636.76--dc22
2006017814

The Leader In Responsible Animal Care For Over 50 Years.™
www.tfhpublications.com

TABLE OF CONTENTS

Chapter

1

HISTORY

Your Pomeranian

In the cold climes of northern Europe, in the regions beneath the Arctic Circle, the Northern Gray Wolf somehow, with man's intervention, produced Dog. These dogs had thick, double-coats for warmth, muzzles sufficiently long to carry the scent of prey to their delicate noses while at the same time warming the air they breathed; erect ears sensitive to even slight, distant sounds, and that were small and fuzzy enough to protect them from frostbite; plus curled tails that lay upon their backs for warmth instead of dragging in the snow and becoming frozen.

The peoples of this Scandinavian region cultivated a working relationship with these hardy, energetic, and intelligent dogs, and soon canine helped human to more efficiently hunt his meals, herd his flocks, and drag his belongings over harsh, frozen terrain. Additionally, they kept each other warm during cold nights and alerted their humans to the presence of possibly dangerous intruders. Eventually, as people of today can attest, companionship developed out of this working bond, and so began the path toward today's Pomeranian.

MOVING SOUTH

The specifics of how the Toy Pomeranian was actually developed is one of history's mysteries. Although true breed types as we recognize them today were not defined as such until the Victorian era, companion and working dogs who were the ancestors of the Pom have been present for several centuries. Out of Lapland, Finland, Iceland, and Siberia, people followed the trade routes around the Baltic Sea to an area of Prussia, bringing with them their Nordic dogs. They settled into Pommern, or the future Pomerania, a land between what is now Germany and Poland. It is likely, that during the Middle Ages, these hardy, useful dogs were introduced into

4000 to 1800 BCE: Nordic peoples and their dogs migrate into Pommern.

800 BCE through 900 CE: The Prussian province sees populations of Slavs, Goths, and varying Teutonic/Germanic tribes evolving into the peoples that would become the Poles; dog types follow the needs of their owners.

1100s CE through early-to-mid-1500s: Region continually shifts between emerging Polish and German provinces and duchies, eventually ending up as part of Germany. At this time, Spitz dogs began to be classified by size.

Germany and Holland through the marauding escapades of Viking warriors into these areas. From here, the perky-eared, bushy–coated dogs spread throughout central Europe and Italy.

In general, these early Pomeranian dogs were white or whitish-biscuit colored. Farther south, they tended to be darker in color, mostly brown, black, or a mix. They weighed about 30 pounds (13.5 kilograms), possibly ranging up to 35 (15.75 kilograms) or even 40 pounds (18 kilograms). These dogs had larger ears and longer muzzles, and were longer in body type than what is typically seen in Nordic breeds of the present.

A SPITZ BY ANY OTHER NAME

In 1540, Count Eberhard zu Sayne is recorded as the first to denote the name "Spitz" for this ever-expanding group of Nordic dogs utilized in Germany as drafters, herders and companions. The word *spitz* in German roughly translates to "sharp point," an apt description for the appearance of this group's head, ears, and face. He also described them as not good for hunting, but devoted to the protection of their owners and homes.

During this time there were many different colors and sizes of dogs, with names related to the region from which they came. They were also divided into types by size and still recognized as such today: Wolfspitz, the giant spitz; Gross Spitz, the large spitz; mittelspitz, the standard, or middle size; Kleinspitz, small; and, Zwergspitz, the dwarf, or toy, size.

The Wolfspitz is sometimes recognized as the Keeshond, called the "overweight Pom" in Holland. The Pomeranian has been known by various names, including the Victorian Pom, the Mini German Spitz,

The Keeshond, a relative of the Pom, is called the "overweight Pom" in Holland.

and in France, the Loulou Poméranie, after a Baltic region where it is believed that some Pom types developed.

Other theories purport that the Pomeranian actually was developed still farther south, in Württemberg, Germany, where, like their northern cousins, they were still used to herd and pull carts. Color differences began to emerge in different regions, with records indicating that by the end of the 17th century, black and brown spitz could be found in Württemberg while large, white Spitz dogs were being cultivated in Pomerania.

No matter where Poms got their start, Great Britain can mostly be credited with the development of the toy dog breed of today. After seeing the dogs in Italy, Queen Charlotte was the first to import white Spitz in 1760 from Pomerania, choosing the region's dogs because of their reputation for quality. The Queen referred to her dogs, Phoebe and Mercury, as Pomeranians, but only because she obtained them there.

In its early show days, smaller Spitz dogs were shown together with larger Spitzes. It wasn't until the late 1800s that they were further classified by weight and the true Pomeranian was established.

Downsizing

During the 1800s, Spitz dogs became quite popular in Britain. These forerunners of today's Pom weighed between 20 and 30 pounds (9 and 13.5 kilograms), and stood about 18 inches (45.7 centimeters) high at the shoulder. These dogs were the first Poms recognized by the Kennel Club in 1870, and allowed to compete in the breed ring.

In 1888, Queen Victoria, probably influenced by her grandmother, Queen Charlotte, brought in some smaller "Pomeranians" from Italy: Windsor's Marco, who was reported to be a 12 pound (5.4 kilogram) red sable; and Gina. Both of these dogs won top honors at dog shows, generating great interest in this tiny version of the Pomeranian.

Victoria also had considerable influence on the development of the breed, both in name and size. Artwork from the period illustrates a preference for the smaller breed, with the Pom depicted as small enough to stand on a book, or being the same height as a garden step.

In their early show days, and for about the next two decades, all sizes of Spitzes were shown together in the same class. The smaller (about 10 pounds or 4.5 kilograms) and more refined looking dogs were referred to as "sports." In 1891, the English Pomeranian Club was founded, and by 1896 was conducting shows for two classes of Pom size: over eight pounds (3.6 kilograms); and under eight pounds, with this distinction eventually being reclassified to seven pounds (3.15 kilograms). It was during this time that the smaller dogs came to be known officially as Pomeranians.

Setting Type

As the popularity of the smaller dogs grew, that of the larger ones declined. The problem was that dogs of both sizes came from the same litters. Breed fanciers of the era tried to establish the tinier Pom by breeding similarly-sized dogs to each other. Despite these initial efforts, the small dogs still produced larger-sized pups, with a variety of sizes showing up in most litters.

Additionally, dogs weighing as little as 3 pounds (1.35 kilograms) were also being born. These "flyweights" were shown along with the larger size Spitzes/Poms, which resulted in a demand for the miniature dogs. Such tiny pups were the exception, as most Poms were born weighing in the typically larger size ranges.

Litters of varying size pups continued to plague breeders during the late Victorian era, but the popularity of the small Poms encouraged their efforts to consistently produce dogs whose adult weight would be less than 10 pounds (4.5 kilograms). By the 1930s, about the time the dog was gaining in popularity in America, repeatable results in setting consistent type finally began to emerge.

HISTORY OF THE POMERANIAN IN THE US

Pomeranians found their way across the ocean to the US during the Victorian era, with the first dog listed with the American Kennel Club (AKC) sometime in the 1880s. The first Pomeranian show in the States took place about 1892. The first Pom registered with the AKC was Dick in 1898, with the breed receiving full recognition in 1900. The first American Pomeranian Club (APC) was founded by Mrs. Frank Smyth and Mrs. Hartley Williamson, and was recognized by the AKC as the breed's parent club in 1909. The Club held its first breed specialty show in 1911.

It didn't take long for the little Pomeranian to capture the hearts of American dog lovers once the breed made its way here from England in the late 1800s.

At that time, AKC show classes were also divided by size: over and under 8 pounds (3.6 kilograms). Breeders in the States, like their British counterparts, had problems maintaining a consistently smaller-sized dog. Just as in Great Britain, the smaller version Pom was the most popular size in the US.

In their efforts to set the standard type of a smaller dog, breeders noticed that white Poms tended to produce larger offspring. Breeding a white Pom to another white Pom not only resulted in larger pups, but the pups also had larger ears and longer muzzles. Consequently, breeders steered away from using white Poms in their programs and mostly used red dogs. Following the fashion of the earlier Victorian fanciers, these reddish dogs increased in favor with lovers of the breed.

Eventually, the breeders' hard work paid off and type became established. The APC's breed standard for 1916 does not describe an ideal size (weight) for the Pom, but a 1935 revision stated that Poms either over or under 7 pounds (3.15 kilograms) were eligible for judging. Regardless of this suggested classification, by the end of the decade, Poms were shown in a single size class. By 1960, the accepted standard defined the correct size as being between 3 to 7 pounds (1.35 to 3.15 kilograms), with the weight range for a show dog set between 4 to 5 pounds (1.8 to 2.25 kilograms).

Royal Dogs

Queen Victoria greatly favored her Pomeranians until her death. One of them, Turi, was at her side when she died in 1901.

Notable Poms

- Westminster Kennel Club's 1988 Best In Show winner CH Great Elms Prince Charming II

- Tucker The Third Muskateer UDX, owner Joyce Hance

- Tiny Tim Pendelton CGC, UD, owner Wendy Donnelly

- First Rally Advanced title earned by Rhett Butler, CDX, RA, owner Dell Brown

- First Rally Excellent title earned by Janesa's Tiffany is an Angel, UD, RE, NA, NAJ, owner Barbara McClatchey

- Top flyball Pom, MACH Lord Peter of Bristol Court, "Keoki," owners John David and Connie Zieba

Although the red dog was seen most frequently at conformation shows, the standard still described Poms of many colors. Permissibility of shading and the acceptance of brindling changed throughout the years to what it is today, but colors of the Pom rainbow have always been varied, and spectators now can see these colors displayed in the show ring.

Whatever shade owners preferred, the Pomeranian has always been one of America's favorite dogs. In the 1930s, registrations for the popular little dog placed him in the top ten most registered breeds. Even throughout both World Wars, fanciers did an admirable job of maintaining the breed, but after WWII, Poms slipped to a lower place in popularity. By 1994 and every year since then, Poms have enjoyed a top-ten spot again, with the AKC registering nearly 40,000 of these cuddly companions each year.

The foxy little Pom is now among the most popular breeds of dogs in the US and around the world, and with looks like these, it's no wonder!

Famous Pom Fanciers

- Martin Luther and Belferlein
- Michelangelo
- Empress Josephine
- Mozart and Pimperl
- Chopin, who didn't have a Pom of his own but enjoyed his friends' dogs so much that he composed a song for them called, "Valse des Petits Chiens"
- Isaac Newton and Diamond, who caused years worth of his research papers to be burned
- Marie Antoinette
- French author Emile Zola
- Several of the dancing Ziegfeld girls
- Liberace
- Television actress Fran Drescher, whose Pom Chester appeared on her show, "The Nanny"
- Rock musician Ozzy Osbourne and his talk show host wife Sharon
- Miss Margaret Hays, owner of one of only two dogs to survive the sinking of the Titanic. She and her Pomeranian escaped into lifeboat seven.

A POSITIVE INFLUENCE

Any breed that has flourished like the Pom has had great breeders working hard to produce beautiful, "typey" (i.e., dogs that follow the standard) healthy dogs for generations to come. For Pomeranians, this includes Viola Proctor, Isadore Schoenberg of Aristic Kennels, and Ruth Beam of Great Elm. Outstanding dogs of the past include Mars, Gold, CH Little Emir, CH Aristic Wee Pepper Pod, and CH Great Elms Little Timstopper.

More recently, such individuals as Dorothy Bonner, Edna Girardot of Scotia Poms, Eleanor Miller of Millamor Kennels, Dolly Trauner, Beverly Norris with Bev-Nor, and Olga and Daryl Baker of Jeribeth Kennels have had a guiding or influential hand developing the breed. Additionally, such breeders as Tim and Sue Goddard of Tim Sue Poms, and Tony Cabrera and Fabian Ariente with Starfire Poms continue to influence the breed with their winning dogs.

CHARACTERISTICS
of the Pomeranian

You want to add a new dog to your family. Once you saw the Pomeranian, you thought this might be the breed for you. This cute and clever breed may just be a good fit for your household, but before you buy a puppy, be sure that you are a good match for each other.

IS A POMERANIAN YOUR PERFECT POOCH?

A Pomeranian can be happy in about any home where he is the focus of admiration and loving attention. The breed's affection for their people is just one of the many characteristics that makes the Pom a great canine companion. But more importantly, can you be a good owner? Can you provide a good home for a Pomeranian?

The first requirement of a good owner is that you believe adopting a dog means that you have made a commitment to that animal for his lifetime. Potential owners should be knowledgeable about dogs in general and learn everything they can about Pomeranians in particular. This means understanding that the Pom requires an extra commitment towards grooming, attention, training, and possibly health care, as well.

People are attracted to Pomeranians because of their adorable, foxy faces, teddy-bear looks, and bright, happy personalities. But all that fur and fun packed into a small dog requires a major investment of time and effort from the owner to care properly for this high-maintenance, demanding breed.

If you pick a Pomeranian as *the* perfect dog for you, it should not only be because you admire their appearance and personality, but also because you are aware of the breed's difficult traits and can accept and live with them.

Fur, Fur, Fur...

According to rescue volunteers, one of the most common reasons Pomeranians are given up is the breed's need for regular grooming. That fluffy coat doesn't get that way without work. Are you ready to spend a few hours every week brushing, combing, clipping, bathing, and drying to maintain that beautiful Pom appearance?

"Pomeranians are cute and adorable, and people may think that because they are a little dog, they won't need much work," says Mary Jane and Dan Coss, Ohio rescue workers, "But they are high maintenance. You have to brush them regularly and keep them clean because they get dirty easily."

Being so fluffy is what attracts people to the Pomeranian; however, his profuse coat and the care it requires are a real commitment from Pom owners.

All that fur can be a haven for fleas too. Are you able to make the effort to keep your yard, home, and dog flea-free? Besides fleas, Pom fur attracts feces, so it is necessary to clean or clip the hindquarters frequently.

When you have that much fur on a dog, there will be lots more fur in the house—on the furniture, the carpeting, and on your clothing. In addition to continual shedding, double-coated dogs such as the Pom also "blow coat." This is a heavier shed that can occur either annually, bi-annually, or whenever the seasons change. Can you live with a dog who sheds constantly, as well as with the mess that the shed fur makes? If the answer is, "no," or "I don't know," don't get a Pom.

...And No Fur

Sometime between the ages of three and five months, Poms lose their baby coat and become very raggedy and scraggly looking, with thin, sparse, wispy, or spiky fur. This phase is called the "uglies" or the "puppy uglies." It can be extreme or dramatic, and last as long as the puppy is growing in his adult coat. Some dogs may experience two full coat losses and regrowths, with males and females experiencing different patterns. It can take anywhere from four to six months for the coat to start filling in, and as long as a year or two for the adult coat to fully develop.

Sometime between the ages of 12 and 20 weeks, Pomeranian puppies lose their baby coats, leaving them with the "puppy uglies."

Poms at a later stage in life may also suffer from extreme hair loss. This is a medical condition for which treatment may or may not be successful in getting the fur to regrow, and your Pom could end up with very little fur; thin, straggly fur and possibly black skin (a medical condition where the skin turns black and fur falls out; see Chapter 8). It's probably better not to get a Pom if you won't be able to love him when he's not beautiful.

Barking, Barking, and More Barking

All dogs bark. Some dogs have a lot to say and bark frequently. Then there's the Pomeranian who really likes to bark. Because he is so alert and in tune with his surroundings, and because he is protective, a Pom feels it is his duty to tell you about every sound, scent, sight, or change of which he becomes aware.

Even among potential owners who are certain the breed's barking will not be a nuisance, rescue workers report that a large number of Poms are returned because they are so "yappy." Additionally, some toy dog breeds, including the Pom, have breathing problems and may snort or cough. Rescue volunteers report that, sadly, some Poms are given up because their owners do not like the sounds they make.

Depending on where you live, it may be important that any dog who stays in your home needs to be quiet. Or you may prefer a dog that doesn't have much to say, or doesn't feel the need to warn you of possible danger. If silence and a quiet, serene atmosphere are essential to you, consider a calmer, less vocal breed than the Pomeranian.

Housetraining

Another main reason that Pomeranians are abandoned is due to problems with housetraining. Breeders and owners experienced with the Pom say that these dogs are "difficult" to housetrain. Why? Possibly because they are so small that they can relieve themselves quickly and leave little evidence of their *faux pas*.

Rescue coordinators also want potential owners to be aware that adopting an older Pom may bring additional problems with indoor soiling. Some Poms who are given up may never have been housetrained at all and may be difficult or impossible to housetrain.

Owners of Poms who have learned not to relieve themselves indoors often recommend the use of a crate to help ensure successful housetraining. Be aware that the training process may take many months to succeed, and owners must unwaveringly adhere to housetraining routines. People who are not comfortable crate training a dog, or who are unable to diligently stick with the plan may do better with a different breed.

If your Pom just doesn't seem to be catching on to housetraining, hang in there. This is a characteristic of the breed that requires patience and persistence.

Even with a thoroughly housetrained Pom there still can be accidents. When the weather is rainy or if he doesn't feel well enough to go out, a Pom may relieve himself inside. Whatever the cause, if having a dog that is not 100 percent reliably housetrained is unacceptable, or if you have flooring that cannot withstand pet accidents, then a Pom is not the dog for you.

Fragile—Handle With Care

Although the Pom is a sturdily built dog, he is nonetheless tiny, with a diminutive body and bones that are fragile and easily broken. Care must always be taken in handling a Pom, and it is essential that he be prevented from jumping off of furniture or out of your arms where landing or falling could cause a serious injury or even death.

Pom owners report that, while they are indoors, they commonly wear soft slippers around their dogs to prevent accidentally stepping on and hurting small feet and legs. Because Poms like to hang out around their people's legs, owners should also learn to do the "Pom shuffle," a walk where you slide your feet across the floor instead of picking them up and setting them down as you normally would.

The Pom is a wonderfully portable breed, but is surprisingly delicate and needs to be handled with care to prevent him from falling.

Despite the fact that the Pom is robust and usually healthy, the breed is disposed to certain health conditions which can be chronic. These conditions, which may include orthopedic problems, tracheal collapse, or tooth loss, can be expensive or time-consuming to treat. Moreover, they may mean a lifestyle change which affects human members of the household in addition to changes for the dog.

Health problems can also result in sleepless nights for owners of sick dogs, cancellation of plans, rearranging schedules to take the dog to the veterinarian, plus the expenditure of funds which may have been planned to pay off debt or for a special weekend get-away. Individuals who lack flexibility in personal and work schedules, or who can't afford extensive veterinary expenses, should consider if they really want to take on a Toy dog with possible health problems.

To breeders, Pomeranians are known as the "heartbreak breed." This is because newborn puppies tend to die quite easily. Part of this is due to small size; puppies who weigh one ounce (28 grams) or less usually die very shortly after birth. Since Poms have small litters,

Poms love to play and be active. Exercise, structured activity, and just plain old doggy games are all good ways to keep this busy breed from getting into trouble. Most Poms are happy playing ball, chase, or tug as long as you or an animal friend are playing along. Surprisingly, many Poms also love to play with water and will happily splash in a small wading pool or even jump in the shower with their human. Whatever you are doing, your Pom is usually happy matching your activity.

there is a chance that all or most of the puppies can be lost. Pups that weigh two ounces or more have a greater likelihood of surviving.

An up side of having a fragile Toy dog is that most tend to be long-lived. The Pom is no exception, with many living an average of 15 or 16 years. Although a Pom may experience arthritis as he ages, other signs of aging may be slower to develop than in some shorter-lived breeds. For people who want their canine companion by their side for many years, the Pom is a good choice.

Household and Environment

Pomeranians can live about anywhere you do. For people who live in small apartments or high-rises, a Pom can be good choice because of his compact size, and because he can be trained to use newspaper or a litterbox. The downside to having a Pom as an apartment dweller is that he does bark frequently and may disturb the neighbors. Poms are also happy living in suburbia or on a farm, though care should be taken to keep your Pom away from large animals and dangerous equipment in a farmyard.

Regardless of where you live, it is preferable to have a fenced yard. Most Poms are not prone to running away, but keeping your dog in an enclosed outdoor play area is far safer for him. Curious Poms may like to explore flower and shrubbery beds, so avoid using poisonous plants or mulch, and consider providing your dog with his own place to dig.

Because of his sledding ancestry, common to all spitz breeds, the Pom does enjoy a good outdoor romp, particularly in the snow. His thick coat insulates him against extremes in temperatures, including hot days. However, many Poms do not like warm weather and become uncomfortably hot during summer. Poms may also disdain going out any longer than necessary if it is raining. Whatever the season, be sure to watch out for the development of "hot spots" (sores caused by licking a spot repeatedly, such as when a flea bite itches or due to allergies; see Chapter 8) in the summer and for tiny feet getting too cold in winter.

Indoors, most any space where you spend time can satisfy the Pom's needs. Homes with multiple stairs or high furniture may present a challenge for a Pom who has a problem with luxating patellas. And because Pomeranians have lots of fur, people who are particular about having a spotless house—with no dog hair on the furniture or floor—might want to consider adopting a different breed.

Family Status

When you choose a dog, one of the most important considerations is the composition of your family and household. Do all family members want a dog? Can everyone contribute to the dog's care? Are they all willing to follow the rules that are set for taking care of and training the dog? If an individual in the household is not thrilled with the idea of getting a dog or is not willing to help with their care, then it might be better not to have a dog as a member of the family.

Are you about to undergo a major life change, such as the birth of a baby, a divorce or wedding, a disruption in work, or a cross-country move? If your family or home life is about to make a major shift, then wait for a more settled time to get a dog—it will be easier for both you and the dog to adapt.

You must also consider your household environment and schedule. Is your home noisy, with loud sounds or rambunctious activity that may upset a Pom and cause nervous or fearful behavior? Are family members healthy enough to accept dog behavior and activity?

Poms and Children

Often people have a preconceived notion that children and dogs are a great combination. While this may be true in some cases, it usually does not apply to Pomeranians and little people. Are the children in your home old enough to respect a dog as a living being and not see him as a toy?

The majority of responsible breeders and rescue groups

Before bringing a Pomeranian home, make sure everyone in the family really wants a dog.

will not place a Pom in a home with children under the age of seven A few impose this restriction if there are children younger than nine years old. The reason is that it's too easy for a small child to accidentally injure a tiny Pom by stepping on him, dropping him, or handling him too roughly. Additionally, some Pomeranians may not be tolerant of active, rowdy, children. The noise they make when running or playing can easily upset, overwhelm, agitate or frighten the sensitive Pom, who may react with nervousness, growling, or snapping.

But there are some families in which Poms and young kids can mix without problems. If the children are well-mannered and understand and abide by the proper guidelines for handling a small dog, and if the Pom is even-tempered and well-socialized, then the combination may work. Just remember: whenever children and dogs are together, they must be supervised constantly. Children should be taught how to play with the dog in a gentle manner, and parents should make certain that the dog is behaving appropriately around the children.

Introducing Kids and Dogs

- Demonstrate with a stuffed toy how to safely and carefully handle a puppy. Have your children practice holding and petting the toy animal before you bring home a dog.

- When your new dog and children meet for the first time, an adult should calmly hold the puppy while the kids quietly and slowly approach, one at a time. Allow the pup to smell the back of their partially closed hand first. Then they may gently pet him.

- Children must not be allowed to handle a Pom roughly. Don't let them pinch or poke him, or pull his tail, ears, or legs. Teach them not step on or drop the dog, or squeeze him tightly.

- Never let your child hit the dog.

- Instruct your children not to stare, bark, or growl at the dog, even if they are only playing. They should leave him alone while he is eating or sleeping, and avoid startling him. This can cause a dog to feel threatened, and he may react by growling, snapping, or biting. Never make a child solely responsible for a dog's care, although they can and should help when they are old enough.

- Show your children, by example, how to nurture and respect your Pom.

Poms and Seniors

Pomeranians can make good companions for retired or elderly persons because the breed loves receiving and giving attention and affection. Elderly owners need to make certain, before bringing home a Pom, that they are physically able to take the dog out to potty or change litter pans or papers, and to keep him groomed and exercised. Another consideration for older folks is the tendency for a Pom to get underfoot. Can they keep themselves from tripping over a small dog and falling, possibly causing injury to both? Poms are a long-lived breed; can provisions be made for their continuing care, should the dog outlive the owner?

Poms and Other Pets

As a sociable animal, most Pomeranians enjoy the company of other animals in addition to their human family. Like most companion animals, a Pom may get along with another pet better if they have been raised together. Additionally, some Pom owners report that their dog gets along well with other household pets such as birds and rabbits.

Cats and Poms can also live happily alongside each other. Preferably, the cat is dog- friendly or will choose not to play with or bother your Pom. In any situation where you are introducing one animal to another, careful supervision is necessary until you are sure that the cat and dog can be together without injuring the other.

Poms like playing with other dogs, particularly those of similar size and personality. However, some Poms prefer only the company of another Pomeranian. When placing a Pom pup or a rescue dog, many breeders and rescue coordinators favor placement in a home where there is already another Pom, as this breed tends to be happier when they are with a companion of the same breed.

In multi-dog households, the pack will form a hierarchy, determining among themselves who is the top dog and so on, down the ranks. To Nordic breeds, particularly those with a sledding background, such as the Pomeranian, pack order is important. Poms quickly sort out the order among themselves, and calm is kept in their pack, with all doggy members respecting their positions and getting along. This preference for orderliness extends to other dog breeds and sizes, as well.

Potential owners need to be extremely cautious about bringing home a Pom if there is a large dog already in the household. A big dog can accidentally cause serious injury or even kill a tiny Pom during rough play. If you want to adopt a Pom and already have a large dog, the larger dog should be calm, gentle-mannered, and friendly with other dogs. Before bringing home your Pom, if possible, try to arrange for the two dogs to meet in a controlled environment to see if they get along. After your Pom comes home and the two dogs begin to live and play together, be certain to always supervise their interaction.

Owners need to be aware that, even though the Pom is small on the outside, inside his head he sees himself as a big, brave, protective dog. Because of this attitude, a Pom may challenge dogs of much larger size without even thinking about his own

Poms make fine companions for older people so long as they can meet the dogs' daily needs for exercise, feeding, and grooming.

Pomeranians especially enjoy the company of other Pomeranians, and also get along well with other animals so long as they are not physically dominated.

tiny stature. It is important to keep your Pom from taking on such dogs. Socialize him so that he understands how to meet new dogs in new situations and keep a watchful eye on him so that you can intervene, should he decide to demonstrate for a strange dog just how tough he thinks he is.

Visitors

Do you have an active social life at home? Or is your home life quiet with few interruptions? Either way, there is no household that doesn't have an occasional knock on the door, whether it's a quick pizza delivery or a guest that plans to stay. If you are going to have a dog, it is important to understand how your dog might react to visitors.

Pomeranians make great therapy dogs because they love to be the center of people's attention. But they don't get that way without training and socialization. You may not plan for your Pom to be a therapy dog, but you do need to plan for having periodic visitors around him in your home.

Some Poms may take naturally to strangers, but many are described by their owners as reserved, stand-offish, or suspicious. Because the Pom is vigilant about watching and supervising his home territory, he is not likely to greet newcomers enthusiastically without first checking them out. Before they even come inside, he will alert you with loud, steady barking to let you know someone is at the door.

Once you let your Pom know that a person is acceptable, or he becomes used to the return of frequent visitors and stops barking his alert, he likely will expect to be the center of your guest's attention as well. Or he may prefer to remain near his person without receiving any pats from your company. Some Poms enjoy being fussed over by friendly strangers, while quite a few others prefer to remain at a watchful distance. Whichever type your Pom is, remember to teach him how to meet and greet new people properly. Respect his choice to socialize with them or not.

A dog who has not been trained to be socially accepting may hide in fear and be miserable whenever visitors arrive. If he has not had any obedience training, he may jump up on your guest, bark at them non-stop, and make them wish they had never visited your home.

Even if your Pom is well-trained and friendly with company, there are some people who do not like and do not want to be around dogs. These people may not continue to visit you, once you add a dog to your family. The reverse is also true. You may want to take your Pom visiting with you, but not everyone will appreciate a doggy guest. Ask before you take your Pom into someone else's home. If you want to meet and hang out with other Pomeranian lovers and their dogs, look for a Pom-specific newsgroup or bulletin board on the internet.

Out and Active

If you are the type of person who spends all your free time in an active sport like cross country skiing, cycling, or canoeing, dreaming of having your dog at your side, then a Pom may not be the best choice for you. Because of his small size and possible orthopedic or tracheal problems, high-impact or endurance sports are not best for this breed.

However, every dog needs regular exercise as part of his care, and because the Pomeranian is a high-energy breed, it is possible to include him in some of your recreational activities. Poms do like to be active with their people, so if you like to hike, walk, or travel to dog-friendly locations in your leisure time, then a Pom might be a good choice for a canine companion.

You needn't rule out getting a Pom if you lead a sedentary lifestyle. A Pom loves to spend time cuddling beside you or in your lap when you sit quietly reading or watching television. His need for exercise can be met with regular walks, a run in the yard, or an indoor

Introducing a New Pet to Your Pack

- The fur can fly when an existing pet meets a new furry member of the family. Start your pack off on the right paw together by following these steps when they first meet.

- If you have a pet who will not accept or cannot get along with a new dog, don't bring in a Pomeranian.

- In households with multiple pets, introduce them one at a time to your new Pomeranian, starting with the alpha (head) dog or cat. Hold the existing dog on leash after placing your new dog in his crate, then allow them to sniff and look at each other while you supervise.

- Once the initial excitement settles down and the existing pet has learned that the new dog is here to stay, it's time to start getting them closer. Have two people present, so that each pet can be more easily controlled while they investigate each other. Until you are absolutely certain that the two animals can interact peacefully, never leave them alone unsupervised.

- Never introduce a new pet at feeding time. Keep them separated while they eat.

- Provide each pet with his own bowl, crate, and bed. Your existing pet needs to be confident that the newcomer will not deprive him of food or steal his prized toys. Without showing favoritism to one pet over the other, make sure that the older pet knows you still love him.

- Don't expect an older pet to accept your new Pomeranian overnight. Introduce them slowly over a period of one to two weeks. But don't rush them into being best friends – acceptance may take longer.

game of chase-the-toy. And an increase in physical exercise could be good for you, also. If you're looking for an activity which allows both you and your Pom some playful exercise, consider getting involved with a competitive dog sport such as rally obedience or agility.

THE POMERANIAN PERSONALITY

Ask people what is so appealing about the Pomeranian, and the list of traits they name seems endless. Enthusiasts cannot sufficiently express in a few words the reasons they adore the Pom personality. Those who have Poms say the breed is addicting and often end up with two, three, or more. They tend to stay devoted to the breed for life.

You will always know when visitors arrive, as your Pom will want to be the first one to greet them at the door.

No Lack of Self-Esteem

The Nordic Spitz-type dogs such as the Alaskan Malamute, Norwegian Elkhound, Siberian Husky, and Samoyed are all breeds that can be described as valiant. The Pom is no exception. In fact, the Pom does not realize that his stature has been shrunk from what it was centuries ago and considers himself no less mighty than his larger cousins.

Surprisingly ready to take on most anything that comes his way, this intrepid little dog is big of heart, long on confidence, and full of a strong sense of self-worth. These traits also help to make him bright, alert, and curious, with a keen intelligence that can lead him into trouble if he is bored. Because the Pom is quite conscious of just how smart and wonderful he is, he prefers to be the focus of attention, the star of the show.

What's Mine Is Mine

Because of his preference for center stage, the Pom can not only be a bit dramatic, he may also be jealous of attention that is focused on other pets, people, or activities. He may place himself between his owner and whatever is taking the focus away from him, then put on a show of his own, dancing around, smiling or "talking" with squeaks, hums, or cat-like sounds in order to regain your attention.

The need to control extends to his home and possessions, so the Pom may also be quite protective over his toys, bowls, bed, or living space. This strong-willed dog also likes the day to go his way and can be quite manipulative at times. With such a strong personality and high energy level, the Pom does best when his busy little mind and body are directed into appropriate doggy activities. Without training and proper handling, it is possible that this pint-sized bully could try to take over your household.

The Strong but Sensitive Type

Although he is independent, the Pom is an affectionate, loyal companion. Whether sleeping in bed with you, scampering at your side while you garden, or traveling on vacation, the Pom enjoys being with his people. Even though he loves your company, he is not a clingy dog.

The Pomeranian is perceptive and intuitive, almost to the point of being uncanny. His keen awareness of his surroundings and his sensitivity to his person's mood makes him a true friend who will stick by your side in good times and bad, responding to the needs of the moment. Despite all the friendship the Pom offers, he is selective when it comes to making friends, with a tendency to be reserved and suspicious when meeting new people. However, given the opportunity, he is usually happy to see repeat visitors who accept his special personality on his terms.

The Downside of Dogs

Life with a dog is a rewarding venture, but it's not problem free. If a Pomeranian is going to be your first experience in the company of canines, be prepared for extra responsibilities and limitations on your lifestyle.

• **Time commitment.** Count on spending at least one hour, but usually two, every day caring for your dog. Having a dog may mean accommodating a schedule for them that's not always convenient for you. Even when you are busy, exhausted, or sick, your dog still needs care.

• **Financial obligations.** Regardless of how well you plan, dogs can cost more than you imagine, and surprise expenses can pop up at times when you can least afford them. When making financial decisions, your dog's needs must come before your personal desires.

• **Legal concerns.** State, county, and municipal laws and ordinances regulate dog ownership in regards to licensing, free-running off-leash dogs, and rabies vaccines. Some cities or developments may limit how many dogs can reside in one household. Owners who violate these laws may be forced to pay fines, have their dog confiscated, or have to cover damages or expenses caused by their dog.

• **Living with dogs is messy.** Pomeranians shed, and you will have fur on your furniture and clothing. Count on cleaning up urine and vomit, and scooping the poop. Dogs leave nose prints on doors, track in mud and grass, and don't put away their toys.

• **Continuing education.** Keeping your knowledge about canine health and behavior current is a never-ending part of the job, and training your dog to always mind his manners is a daily effort.

• **Constant supervision.** You must always be vigilant to keep your dog safe and out of harm's way. Know where he is and what he is doing at all times.

On some days, dog ownership can be trying and tedious. However, this doesn't mean it's all right to trade in your dog for an easier "hobby." First-time owners should be aware that caring for puppies, sick, injured, elderly, or special-needs dogs is not easy. Should the human-canine relationship get rough, it's not acceptable to abandon your dog. A commitment to a Pomeranian is a commitment for life.

Don't let their small size make you think Poms don't enjoy the great outdoors. They love a good romp as much as a bigger dog.

A Final Caution

Because the Pomeranian is such a popular dog, there are many people who breed and sell puppies just to make money, without a vigilant eye towards the health or temperament of these pups. Responsible breeders and rescue volunteers advise people searching for a Pom to be careful where they obtain a puppy, as many of these poorly-produced dogs are fearful, snappy, or downright neurotic. Additionally, careful observation has shown that nearly all of the Poms from second-rate breedings tend to develop luxating patellas, collapsing tracheas, or both.

Also keep in mind that dogs bred strictly as companions and for their appearance may be less similar in breed personality traits than some other breeds which are bred for specific functional characteristics. For example, a herding breed like the Border Collie will have similar personalities because they have been bred to perform the same function. But Pomeranians who have been bred for company and cuddling tend to have a broader range of personality traits—and differences.

"Once you have a breed that has been bred more for cuteness

and companionship, their temperaments and personalities may be so varied that you can't really state that they have a personality that is unique to the breed," says Pom enthusiast Mary Felkins, "When it comes to Poms, I have found their personalities to be very different from each other. In my opinion, they have a temperament that may be more environmentally induced.

"I feel that it's more for what the Pom looks like that draws most people to the breed, and sometimes we tend to overlook a temperament or personality that might not be as adorable as the dog himself," Felkins illustrates. "However, most well-cared-for small dog breeds are going to have similar personalities. And because people treat Poms differently —more child-like and nearly always kept indoors—Poms tend to be more people oriented."

PUTTING TOGETHER A POMERANIAN

All breeds have a recognized description and the Pomeranian is no exception. The official standard of this breed begins with a general description of his appearance and moves on to describe his various parts as well as his motion and personality.

At a Glance

The opening to the official Pomeranian breed standard used to be short, summarily noting the dog's overall shape and look, with an even shorter reference to character. Today's introduction provides a condensed but complete description of everything Pom – shape, size, fur, personality, and more.

Once defined as "cobby" and "closely-coupled," these terms have been changed to the more easily understood terms of "compact" and "short-backed," presenting a picture of an energetic

Do Your Research

When selecting a Pomeranian as a canine companion, whether for looks, personality, or both, take the advice of Central Ohio Poms and More Rescue Coordinator Linda Simmons, and "Research, research, research," before making a final purchase.

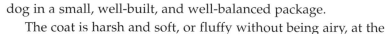

dog in a small, well-built, and well-balanced package.

The coat is harsh and soft, or fluffy without being airy, at the same time. This combination results in fur that is thick, luxuriant, and full-bodied. While fur on the tail is different, it is lush and feathery, carried gracefully on the back.

Heavy emphasis is placed on summarizing the ideal Pom character since these dogs serve as companions. Poms should exhibit intelligence and have a bright appearance, keenly aware of and curious about their surroundings, but generally happy in disposition. While cheerful in nature, the Pom is not a pushover, but a dog that should possess a compelling presence. The perky personality should carry into the walk, showing liveliness in a dog that is sure-footed and fit, regardless of size.

Standards to Breed By

The dictionary defines "standard" as a model, approved by an authority source, used as a foundation against which other representations are compared. This is true when applied to the breed standards for all purebred dogs. The American Kennel Club explains that the studious comprehension of a breed should start with that breed's standard.

These standards are prepared by people with a long history and experience in their breed, and describe what the perfect specimen of that dog should be. This description covers structure, movement, type, and temperament. Since no dog is perfect, the standard is used as a template for breeding and judging the ideal dog, and for producing future generations of healthy, happy companion animals.

Three Dimensions

Most breed standards give an ideal weight range to describe the size of a dog, and the Pom is no exception. They may be as tiny as 3 pounds (1.35 kilograms), or as "large" as 7 pounds (3.15 kilograms). The ideal Pom should weigh in at between 4 and 6 pounds (1.8 and 2.7 kilograms), a median that strives to keep the breed the same size over passing generations.

Without the weight guidelines, Pomeranians could revert back to the larger size of their ancestors from which they were bred down to today's Toy size. It is also possible to go too far in the other direction and breed dogs who are miniscule. Producers of Poms that do not breed with an eye toward the standard may offer puppies who grow to be a "huge" 12 to 18 pounds (5.4 to 8.1 kilograms), or as tiny as 2 pounds (.9 kilogram). The standard clearly states that dogs who are too small or too large should not be considered for showing, much less breeding.

More importantly, however, the size section places greater emphasis on judging, as a whole, a Pomeranian who has many outstanding traits, such as expression, gait, and coat combined, rather than on size alone.

The dimensions detailed in the standard define a dog whose

back is slightly shorter in length than the dog is tall. The Pom's frame should be medium, neither too fine nor too heavy, with the legs and head being proportionate to the size of the body. Although this is a toy dog that may appear fine and fragile, touching the frame beneath the fur should reveal a body that has substance.

Despite a standard that describes the size and substance of the body, different breeders and judges may interpret this description as different ideals. As a result, fanciers describe two types of Pomeranians. The teddy-bear type is rounder, with a more open face, and may have a shorter muzzle. This type also has heavier bone structure. A foxy type is a Pom that is more like the original, pointy Spitz appearance, with a longer muzzle, tighter facial features, and lighter build.

The standard for the breed describes the Pom as compact, well-balanced, and with a compelling presence.

Front to Back and In Between

The Pom standard repeatedly notes the balance and proportion the breed should have, starting with the head. Although two facial types exist, the muzzle is defined as somewhat short, but it is also clear that despite the breed's foxy face, a Pom should not have an excessively elongated nose lacking in substance beneath the eyes. The face should be enhanced with a look that is bright, inquisitive, and engaged—alert.

Head shape should curve gracefully but shouldn't be so round that the skull resembles the cupola of a capitol building. Poms with such a domed head are not considered acceptable for showing or breeding. If an imaginary line were drawn from nose to eyes to ears, it would form a triangle, defining an ideal, wedge-shaped head.

Ears are tiny and set on the top of the head, and the eyes should be dark, luminous, and slightly elongated at the corners, rather than round. Nose and eyelids are black, but dogs who are darker

The Pom's tiny ears are set on top of his head, his eyes are dark and slightly elongated, and his nose and eyelids are the same shade of black, brown, or gray.

brown or grayish have noses to match. For a breed that may be prone to dental problems, a correct bite is important. Teeth should close together like blades on a pair of scissors. While it isn't critical if a single tooth is misaligned, teeth that do not align correctly can be a serious problem.

As befits a toy dog, the Pom's back is compact as is the neck, which is positioned so that the head is carried erect, contributing to his alert look. Despite his body's tiny size, the Pom's ribcage should feel substantial (not thin or fragile), as well as widely set and moderately deep.

At one time, the Pomeranian's tail was curled tightly over the back like his Nordic ancestors. But as the breed evolved, the tail gradually uncurled. The tail on today's Pom is full and feathered, but lies open on top of the back.

An affectionate and loyal companion, your Pom will soon be an adored family member.

Getting Around

Front legs that point neither in nor out are set into shoulders that are balanced in proportion, emphasizing the proud carriage of the breed. Feet are tiny and arched, as if the dog is standing on his toes. The ankle area should not be weak or "sag." The rear legs are balanced with those in front, with the hip behind the tail. Back legs are also straight and well built, with portions being at a 90-degree angle to the floor. Like front legs, back legs are also strong, without weakness.

The Pom should appear animated and lively when walking briskly. Movement should appear fluid, without bounce or unnecessary motion. Legs should reach effortlessly for the next step, with front and rear legs moving in smooth harmony. As in many breeds, the front and rear feet on diagonal sides should meet underneath the center of the body. The Pomeranian should look as balanced in motion as in still profile.

A Coat of Many Colors

Like all of his Nordic relatives, the Pomeranian has a heavy double coat. First is an undercoat which, as the name implies, is

The Pomeranian has a fluid, animated movement.

the somewhat hidden fur beneath the more obvious exterior coat. This undercoat should be shorter, very thick, and plush to the touch. The fur of the outercoat is longer, without curl or wave, and should have body. Although the undercoat is what makes the outercoat fluff away from the dog's body, the exterior fur—the guard hairs—should have substance of their own. The quality of the fur should help protect the dog from inclement weather. The coat should never appear dull; rather, it should have a natural sheen.

Fur should be the longest and most dense around the neck, shoulders, and chest. Coat length on the legs is much shorter, but is still dense, with some feathering. On the tail, the fur is much longer, but not as thick, and should flow with the lay of the tail. A Pom should never have fur that lies flat or is too soft from lack of body. The under- or outercoats should also not be too thin or sparse—an open coat—which is a fault in appearance, feel, and purpose.

Many people are used to seeing the Pomeranian in warm or pale orange to red shades. But in actuality the breed has many colors, all of which are permitted in the show ring. Solid colors incorporate varying shades of orange, cream, sable, black, rich brown and/or pale beaver, and blue, a rare grayish shade. Mixed colors include the black and tan pattern, where pale brownish highlights occur on the nose, chest, neck, and eyebrows, and brindle, which is darker striping found on a medium shade dog. Additionally there are Parti Poms, which are primarily white with the addition of areas of other solid colors in places like ears, tail, legs, and so forth. A show quality Parti should have white down the center of the face.

Personality Plus

As a companion dog, possibly the highest requirement of the Pomeranian is personality. The breed's standard is very clear that this dog should be sociable, smart, and full of *joie de vivre*. This combination is largely responsible for the Pom's prized position as best friend and dog show winner. Overall, the standard defines a dog that, despite its diminutive size, should possess the physical, emotional and behavioral stability, and stamina of its larger cousins.

Colors of the Pom

Solid
- Orange
- Cream
- Sable
- Black
- Brown
- Blue

Mixed
- Black & Tan
- Parti

Few dogs can match the spunky little Pomeranian's joie de vivre.

PREPARING
for Your Pomeranian

After careful, thorough consideration, you've made the decision to get a dog. You've determined that you have the time, energy, budget, and patience essential for a lifelong commitment to a canine companion. You've also decided it's a Pomeranian you want—you know that their looks and personality appeal to you more than any other breed. You believe that the extra effort of grooming, training, and providing health care for a Pomeranian are worth it. And you're willing to learn all the information you need in order to provide a dog with the best home possible.

WHICH POMERANIAN SHOULD YOU PICK?

Before finding the Pom of your dreams, a few more decisions are necessary—those of age, gender, and where to find your dog.

Boy or Girl?

First you need to consider if you want a male or female. Each is lovable and loving in return, but there are subtle differences. Although each dog's personality is unique, in general females may be prissier and moodier, while males may be rowdier and more ornery. Both are affectionate, but while males are unashamedly sweet about cuddle time, females can be more independent and demanding of affection on their own terms. Each gender will have its own housetraining issues to overcome, but males tend to spray and mark, and intact females will have heat cycles. Overall differences are minor, and both males and females make wonderful companions.

Puppy or Adult?

One of the biggest decisions you'll have to make is whether to get a puppy or an adult dog. Both older dogs and younger pups require your time, attention, and love, but the similarities stop there. Puppies tug at your heart strings with their extra cute looks and mannerisms. Those same mannerisms are what make them a handful to

Think carefully about whether you want to bring a puppy or an adult Pom into your home. Both of these dogs are irresistible.

raise. They cry, chew, bark, get into trouble, and they need to be fed and taken out to potty nearly every time you turn around. They have to be trained, constantly supervised, and are a never-ending job the first few months of their lives. With puppies, many owners can't wait for them to grow up and out of trouble, but when they are grown, these same owners miss their dog's puppyhood.

Although adult dogs also require care, they don't demand the constant attention that a puppy does. They tend to have more training and manners already in place. With a mature dog, you know exactly what you're getting, which is not always the case even with a wisely chosen, well-bred puppy. You can train growing puppies into the behavior that you expect of them. Adults may need some refresher training when it comes to manners, but they already have developed their own behaviors. Consider both options and decide which age fits best into your family and schedule, and for whom you can provide the best home. Whatever your preference, an adult Pom usually will bond to his new family as closely as a puppy would.

Competitor or Companion?

Is your Pomeranian going to be the star of your home, or do you have hopes that he will be a star in the conformation show ring? Either will be a loving companion, but the conformation Pomeranian will require extra expenses, training, time, and effort to embark on a show career. Choosing a show-quality Pom requires more research, planning, and expense. If you think you might want to try strutting your dog's stuff in conformation competition, look for breeders who have bred multiple champions. Talk to them at length, and enlist their aid in choosing the right show puppy for you.

Male or female, puppy or adult, show or pet, remember that, when looking for the perfect Pomeranian for your home, each dog is an individual. Genetics, environment, and training will all affect the development of his personality, but each makes for a special, unique companion to love.

Once you've figured out which type Pomeranian is the best fit for your lifestyle, a most important criterion is still to be considered: where will you get your dog? There are always so many puppies and dogs for sale, adoption, or give-away that the choices can be overwhelming. Ads on the internet, in magazines and local newspapers; breeders and dog farmers; rescue groups; shelters; dog pounds; and even pet stores or owner give-ups … how do you choose a safe, reputable resource for obtaining your family's pet?

PURCHASING A PUPPY

Breeders

Finding a reliable source for your Pom puppy needs to be your main priority. A conformation show is one of the first places to look for a good source and see quality Poms in action at the same time. Breeders and handlers will be present who can answer your questions about the breed (after they are done showing), breeding programs, available puppies, and planned litters. At the show, catalogues can be purchased that list the names and addresses of owner-breeders so that you can contact them later. Find a show near your area by contacting the AKC or checking the AKC events calendar online at www.akc.org/events/.

Breeders may also be found online and through national dog magazine listings. But web pages and nationally published advertising do not necessarily mean that the source is reputable and the puppies are sound. To determine if a breeder can provide you with a healthy, happy-tempered puppy, there are many questions you need to ask. When asking questions, keep in mind that a good breeder does not breed for income, but for the betterment of the breed. In actuality, reputable breeders tend to lose money on their litters because their work is about the puppies, not about profit.

A dog show is a good place to meet breeders, who frequently bring more than one dog to compete, making it easier for you to see the differences among them.

Questions to ask a potential breeder focus on the dogs' health history and the purchase policies. How many generations back in a litter's pedigree have health histories been checked and cleared? For what genetic defects does the breeder test and strive to eliminate? Due to the presence of certain inherited diseases and conditions in the Pom, parents, grandparents, and preferably great-grandparents should have been examined, cleared, and if applicable, had the test results registered with OFA (Orthopedic Foundation for Animals) or CERF (Canine Eye Registration Foundation).

If the breeder is close to your area, arrange a visit so you can see the puppies in their home environment. It will also give you a chance to see the dam and get information about the sire. If a breeder doesn't want you to come, this could be a signal that there are problems that are being hidden. If the breeder is too far away to visit, ask them to send pictures of the mother, pups, and kennel.

Find out the condition of the mother and the puppies: are they all healthy? Are the dogs and their area clean and well-kept? What type of a health guarantee does the breeder provide? Is she (or he) willing to take the puppy back or assist you if there are problems? Are puppy prices reasonable for the quality of the litter? Are the prices too low or too high, or comparable to prices charged by other reputable breeders? Ask for references from previous puppy buyers.

In return, be prepared to be interrogated by the breeder. Expect to provide personal character references. If the breeder doesn't ask you questions, this could be a sign of someone who doesn't care where the puppies go or how they will be cared for—and a warning of how little effort went into planning the litter.

Beware of Bad Breeding

Despite the appeal of a puppy face that promises you love, buying a puppy from a source with a less than sterling reputation is an almost certain promise of heartbreak in days to come. Signs that you should look for a different source might include:

- Breeder has several types of dogs, lots of puppies or has many litters every year.

- Advertises only in small or local newspapers, neighborhood newsletters, or only on internet sites that too easily list dogs for sale to anyone that has the money.

- Puppies under eight weeks of age who are described as "ready to go."

- Prices that are too low to be believable. And, unless you're buying a very special show-quality dog, high prices that are not an indication of an exceptional dog, just of exceptional greed.

- No contract is offered or required, or contract terms that make you uneasy.

- The source is not insistent on having puppies returned, or explicitly tells you she will not take the puppy back should you be unable to keep him.

- The mother or the puppies are shy, fearful, nasty tempered, in poor condition, or appear sick or listless. Also, if the mother cannot be viewed or if information about the father is withheld, the breeder is probably hiding something.

- AKC papers are unavailable, which could point to a problem with the breeder.

- Breeder won't provide you with client references, withholds data about health or history, or blatantly denies the existence of noticeable health problems.

- Breeder does not actually have the dam, sire, or puppies on site, only buys puppies from other "breeders" and resells them, usually via the internet, offered as a puppy locator service.

Don't be offended when she or he thoroughly quizz you about your dog knowledge and experience, your family, lifestyle, finances, and living facilities. A caring breeder will ask about your ability to provide for a puppy, your plans for the puppy, if your home and family are suitable both physically and emotionally for a puppy, and if you will make a lifetime commitment to the welfare of a new dog.

When you and the breeder satisfy each other's requirements and a special puppy has picked you out, the sale of a purebred Pomeranian should come with a detailed contract. Terms should include your obligations towards the puppy and the return of the dog if you no longer can provide a good home, along with a spay/neuter agreement, and the details of the purchase. The breeder should also provide you with a complete veterinary and vaccine record, a copy of your puppy's pedigree, and an AKC form for registering your puppy (more information on registration follows in this chapter).

Reputable breeders who care about dogs will care about your puppy for his lifetime. Keep in touch with her or him if you have questions about or problems with your Pom. Chances are good that she or he will try to help.

No matter where you get your dog, a healthy puppy looks like, well, like he's healthy. He should have:

- A shiny coat
- Bright, clear eyes
- A happy expression
- Pink gums and tongue
- An active energy level
- Firm stools of a normal color
- That indefinable puppy glow and sweet puppy breath

A puppy should NOT have:

- Runny eyes or nose
- Droopy posture
- Lethargic appearance
- Dull coat
- Other signs that make you immediately think, "Ooh that puppy looks sick."

Pet Stores

You're running errands. As you walk to your car, you pass a pet shop. You weren't thinking about buying a puppy today, but you go in just to look. And there's a Pomeranian, smiling at you and begging you to take him home. What do you do? Just like obtaining a puppy from any other source, there are questions you need to ask and information you need to obtain.

The first consideration is health. Does the puppy look healthy? Are his eyes clear and bright, free from discharge, without glassy appearance? Are his ears clean, without waxy buildup or redness? Does he have a discharge from his nose? Is he coughing, sneezing, or vomiting? Does he have diarrhea? Is the belly distended or have a bulge? Does his coat look healthy, or is it dull looking? Are his legs straight? Does he walk with a limp? Is he active without being hyper? If the puppy does not appear healthy, don't take him home.

Next, what kind of guarantees and contracts does the store offer? If a problem arises with the puppy, what will the store do to help remedy the situation? Ask for a health guarantee with the same stipulations you would request from a breeder. Be certain that the guarantee does not have exclusions that would normally be covered by a breeder.

Before giving in to your impulse to buy that adorable Pom in the window, get all the information about him. Ask the store to provide documented information about the puppy's breeder and his health, and about shipping history to the store. Ask the sales clerk about registrations, breed characteristics, behavior, and exposure to training or socialization. If you feel you don't receive a satisfactory answer, ask them to obtain more data for you from a good reference source. Ask for copies of the puppy's health, worming, and vaccination history and the breeder's contact information. Get any related paperwork, such as registration papers, contracts, and warranties, and read them before signing on the dotted line.

What are the store's return policies? If the puppy has a health or behavior problem, or your situation changes and you can no longer keep the puppy, will they rehome the puppy for you or contact the breeder and make arrangements for her to take him back? Ask for references of customer's who are satisfied with their pet-shop purchase.

Regardless of how deeply you may have fallen head over heels for a pup in a pet store, if any of the terms of the sale are unacceptable, if any information is unclear or makes you feel uncomfortable, do not buy the puppy. Buying any dog from any source about which you are not 100 percent certain is not the way to find a loving canine companion.

REGISTERING YOUR POMERANIAN

American Kennel Club (AKC)

Owners who purchase a puppy that qualifies for AKC registration should receive documentation from the breeder that the litter has been registered, including the sire and dam's registration numbers. Additionally you should be given a registration form to complete and mail to the AKC. It is now possible to register most puppies online at www.akc.org/dogreg/.

You will need to choose a "registered" name for your Pom—a name that is longer and more formal than his "call" name—usually one which includes the breeder's kennel name. Additional information which the form requests is the name and address of the owner, sire and dam's names and numbers, birth and registration dates, breed, color, and gender information. Registrations may be full or limited. Limited registration means that no litters born as a result of breeding your dog can ever be registered, whether you own the sire or the dam, and that the dog is not eligible for conformation showing. However, a dog with a limited registration is still fully recognized and able to legitimately participate in other AKC dog competition events, such as obedience, and have the records of his competition maintained by the AKC.

Caveat Emptor

Purchasing any Pomeranian will go more smoothly if you carefully consider each option about from whom and where you buy a dog. Over your Pom's lifetime, the effort put into first researching your purchase or adoption will pay off with a healthier, more even-tempered dog in the long run. Because dogs are family members who experience emotional and physical pain when there's a problem with them, it's not the same as when something goes wrong with an appliance or automobile. When your dog hurts, you hurt; you can't just "repair" or replace a dog and move on without consequence.

As the old cliché goes, "buyer beware," even when it comes to purchasing a dog. Be absolutely convinced that you are getting the right dog from the right provider before you make the commitment to buy or adopt. Don't overlook provisions in a contract that aren't what's best for you and your future puppy. If you need or are promised paperwork regarding your dog, keep asking until you get it. Don't neglect to ask questions because you don't want to risk offending someone who has a Pomeranian available.

The Kennel Club (KC)

Registry for a dog is done through the Kennel Club (the British counterpart to the AKC) when you purchase a Pomeranian puppy in the United Kingdom. At the time a litter is born, the breeder registers the pups. When you purchase one of those puppies, you are given a KC certificate of registration and ownership. The breeder provides a portion of this form, which then needs to be filled out and submitted by the new owner. Completion and acceptance of this form transfers ownership of the registered puppy. Ownership must be transferred before a new owner can participate in any Kennel Club regulated dog sporting events. More information can be found at www.the-kennel-club.org.uk.

ADOPTION OPTIONS

Rescue

There are several options if you've decided you would like to adopt an adult Pomeranian. You can check with breeders to see if they have a retired show dog they would like to place. These dogs are most often outgoing, healthy dogs just looking for a retirement home away from the ring. Nevertheless, ask the same questions you would if you were looking for a puppy.

Breed rescue is another option for finding a Pomeranian in need of a good home. Rescue groups are organized by individual Pom enthusiasts who have a thick skin and soft hearts, generous purse strings, extra space in their homes, tireless

Healthy puppies, like these, should have bright, clear eyes; clean, lustrous fur; and an overall look of well-being.

patience, and plenty of experience caring for and retraining dogs. Abandoned or surrendered by owners, removed from shelters, or picked up by concerned animal lovers, these needy Poms are placed into temporary foster homes. In foster care, they receive veterinary testing, any needed treatment, including vaccination and neutering, if necessary, and are trained and socialized. Additionally, to ensure a good match in a new permanent home, their temperaments are evaluated to see if they get along with children, other animals, and what type of people they like or dislike. These dogs are loved by the people with whom they are temporarily living.

When you purchase a purebred puppy, you receive a registration form that you need to complete and send to the registering organization before your puppy is officially registered.

Sadly, Pomeranian rescue usually has more dogs than there are qualified homes. The primary reasons for abandonment or surrender are often owners who can't deal with housetraining issues, health problems, frequent barking, or who are just incapable of providing the care and attention this breed requires. Other reasons include divorce, loss of income, a forced move to a new location where pets aren't permitted, death in the family, or simply owners who cannot cope with dog behavior in general. Whatever the reason, there are many wonderful Pomeranians in rescue—one that may be just right for you.

Rescue dogs are usually 7 months of age and older, with most being middle-aged (3 to 7 years) to seniors (7 years and up). Not all dogs in breed rescue will be 100 percent purebred, but in most groups they will be at least half Pomeranian. Some come with health conditions that require treatment; others have training or minor behavior issues that need work. Dogs with serious problems like biting are seldom offered for adoption through ethical rescue groups.

Adopting a Pom from a rescue group may not be the best option for everyone. Rescuing a dog takes extra time, attention, and maybe money. But for those who are able to provide a special dog that extra care, rescues reward the effort with gratitude and love, as most tend to bond very deeply to their new families.

There are plenty of adult Pomeranians who can make exceptional companions, and who need a home.

To find a rescued Pomeranian, search the internet for the group closest to your area. Ask the same questions you would if you were buying a puppy from a breeder. While much of the dog's background may never be known, get as detailed a recent history as possible from the foster volunteer. Let the rescue coordinators guide you in selecting a dog that is best suited for your home and lifestyle.

Rescue dogs cannot be adopted for free. Just because they were another person's cast off does not mean that they are without value or expense. Adoption fees are typically higher than in shelters, but are less than the purchase price of a puppy, and are used to cover the costs of fostering, placement and medical expenses, which can often be extensive.

As a potential owner, you will be required to fill out an application that helps determine if you can provide a suitable, loving home for the remainder of the dog's life. Questions will be asked about your experience with dogs and the breed, why you want a Pomeranian, your financial ability to provide care, your family size, activities, and schedule, yard and household facilities, and much more. In many cases, a volunteer will come to your home for a pre-qualification interview. Standards set by the groups

People who help older dogs find new homes are as diligent about background checks as are puppy sellers. These dogs need new forever homes.

for potential owners are very high. Don't let this upset you—the goal of the rescue group is to make as perfect and permanent a match as possible so that a Pomeranian once rescued should never be in need of rescue again.

Animal Shelters

According to the Humane Society of the United States, nearly 25 percent of dogs in animal shelters are purebreds. Can a Pomeranian end up in a shelter? Yes, all too often, and for the same reasons they end up in rescue.

If you are thinking about searching for a Pom in a shelter, keep in mind that the background of the dog may be virtually unknown. Shelter workers will give what information they have, but this may be limited to where the dog was picked up or if an owner turned him in. In an

Ask a lot of questions and choose your Pom with your head and not just your heart.

owner give-up, the true reason for surrender may not have been given to the shelter. The dog's medical history, other than while in the shelter, will probably also be unknown. Before you adopt a Pom from a shelter, make sure you are prepared and able to deal with extensive medical or behavioral issues. Shelter dogs can turn out to be special-needs dogs.

While some people may view a pound puppy as a nightmare waiting to happen, maybe you are a potential owner who would consider a Pom from a shelter to be a wonderful surprise. It is possible to find the Pomeranian of your dreams in a shelter, if you are willing to work with the shelter employees and to invest the time, money and effort needed to transform your new Pom into a loving companion. Just like Pom's from rescue groups, those who have been pulled from a shelter into a caring home often seem to express their gratitude by bonding closely with their new people.

To find a shelter in your area, check the phone directory or with your county services administration offices. Shelter and rescue dogs can both be found through www.petfinder.com and www.pets911.com.

PUPPY PREP YOUR HOME

You've found the perfect puppy, and he'll be coming home

in a few days. Now you need to get your home ready for the big day. Because of their bright, inquisitive personalities, Pomeranian puppies can be adept at getting into trouble, chewing dangerous objects, or shredding personal belongings that are off limits to tiny teeth. In a matter of minutes, a single, small pup can cause hundreds, even thousands of dollars worth of damage and seriously injure himself in the process.

Identify His Space

Position baby gates across doorways into areas where your puppy isn't allowed. Close cabinets, drawers, and doors to rooms or storage spaces where he could get into trouble. Since a puppy believes that it's okay to chew anything that is within reach, provide plenty of toys for his busy little mouth (read more about training not to chew in chapter 6). Always keep a close eye on what he is doing, no matter how well you have prepared your home for his arrival.

If you don't want your Pom's first days in your home to be a series of reprimands, ("No. Get out of there. Leave that alone. Stop it. Drop that. No.") then puppy-proof your house and yard before he arrives. Think of it as child-proofing your home, except that your puppy is smaller and more active than a baby and has easier, quicker access to items at his level.

Puppy-Proof the Home Environment

Pick up, put out of reach, secure, or keep your Pom away from:

- Electrical and telephone cords or wires, computer cables;
- Drawstrings from draperies or blinds, throw pillows, arm covers from chairs, throw rugs;
- Television and other remote controls, DVDs , CDs, video or cassette tapes;
- Knick-knacks, figurines or collectibles, candles, potpourri, air fresheners including the plug in types;
- Houseplants, some of which are poisonous, including dead leaves;
- Medications, drugs, toiletries, cosmetics, combs, toothbrushes, hair ribbons or scrunchers, hair pins, jewelry;
- Heavy items like lamps that can get pulled down or knocked over onto your tiny Pom;
- Food, crumbs, bones or discarded cooking items, candy dishes, puppy's own food and treats in which he could overindulge;
- Garbage and trash cans or bags, debris from fireplaces, firewood and kindling;
- Pens, pencils, crayons, markers, paper clips, rubber bands, tacks, staples, tape, paper shredding machines, books, magazines, mail, newspapers, important documents and money (paper or coin);

- Paper towels and napkins, tissues, toilet paper, roll cores, cleaning items, rags, sponges, household chemicals, detergents;
- Dirty laundry, shoes, socks, hats, scarves and gloves;
- Tools, nails, string, fasteners, glue, crafting and sewing items, scissors;
- Children's toys, sporting equipment, hunting or fishing gear.
- Large items that cannot be moved out of reach, like chair- or table legs, cabinet doors, doorstops, or corner trim which can be treated with a product that discourages chewing.
- Because attics, garages, and basements may contain so many hazardous objects, it's usually best to keep your puppy out of these rooms at all times.

Once you've puppy-proofed the inside of your home, prepare the yard area to which your Pom will have access.

- Check fencing for weak or broken areas where your puppy could escape. Make necessary repairs and secure the bottom of the fence to the ground. Put padlocks on fence gates.
- Remove poisonous shrubs and flowers. Also remove any cocoa mulch; it has an appealing odor but can be toxic if ingested.
- Avoid the use of fertilizers, pesticides or herbicides on the ground in your puppy's area, if at all possible. These chemicals can be absorbed through the skin of the feet, or licked off the fur, which

Selecting the pup or puppies for you and your family is just the beginning. Now it's time to prepare your home for the new arrivals.

Carefully inspect your home and your yard for anything your curious puppy may find that could potentially harm him.

can result in serious poisoning or death. If you must treat your puppy's area with any of these chemicals, keep him off the lawn for at least 48 hours afterwards or until after a steady, rinsing rain.

• Don't leave gardening tools or mowing equipment in your puppy's part of the yard.

• Keep your puppy away from your swimming pool or pond.

• Scoop the poop from your puppy's potty zone!

When you think your home is a puppy-proof zone, go through each area again. Did you miss anything? Are there objects in which your puppy could get caught or that he could pull down or rip up? Ask yourself, "If I were a puppy, would this be an interesting place to explore? Would this be fun to chew or shred?"

Once your house and yard are safe for your young Pomeranian, set up his crate and bowls in the area designated for him. Then when you introduce him to his new environment, he should settle happily into his new home.

SUPPLIES

If you like to shop, then getting ready to bring home your new Pom is a perfect reason for a shopping expedition. You and your home will be better prepared for your new pal if you purchase the following items for him:

• Books with breed-specific information, a home-medical reference for dogs, puppy care, training, and canine behavior books.

• Food, food and water bowls (two sets), food storage containers. Bowls should be Pomeranian-sized and easy to clean. Stainless steel is the preferred choice of many breeders, but you may opt for a decorative ceramic style instead. Plastic bowls are not the best choice for light-colored or white Poms, as it may be possible for some of them to discolor the dog's coat. But if plastic is what you prefer, try to select a heavy, durable bowl that is chip and peel resistant, and is dishwasher safe.

• Crate, crate padding, and bed—possibly use old blankets or towels. The crate should be just large enough for your dog to stand up and turn around. It's all right to buy his adult-sized crate now, but block off the extra room with a crate divider until he's fully grown. Plastic, wire, and soft-sided crates are all good models. Just be careful that your pup can't get through or get caught in any openings between wires. Plastic should be chew-resistant and soft-sides should not have any zippers or objects inside which your puppy could chew off and then swallow. Latches should be escape resistant.

- Toys and chew toys. Look for toys that are safe for puppies, with no small pieces or parts that are easily removed and on which he could choke. Chewables should resist splintering.
- Puppy collar and leash, identification tag. Be careful in choosing a collar for your Pom as most collars may cause the fur on his neck and ruff to mat. A harness and leash combo may work best for walking your Pomeranian as a standard collar-leash may damage a trachea already prone to collapsing.

Separate food and water bowls are just some of the supplies your new puppy or dog will need.

- Healthy, bite-sized treats for training and rewards.
- Baby gate; possibly an exercise pen. Select a style that your dog won't easily knock down or over which he could climb or jump.
- Cleaners, disinfectants, odor neutralizer, air freshener, and enzyme carpet cleaner. Consider getting a hand-held spot cleaning machine.
- Pooper-scooper tools including plastic collection bags, old newspapers, possibly puppy pads
- Paper towels, small indoor garbage bags.
- Puppy-resistant indoor trash cans (ones that are difficult to open, or childproof).
- Grooming tools and supplies (see chapter 5); towels for drying puppy if he gets wet outdoors.
- Basket or container for storing puppy's toys and supplies when not in use.

• Primary Identification: "Primary" identification is readily seen by anyone who finds the dog, and no special equipment is necessary to locate or read the identifier. Engraved tags are the main way to provide primary ID for your dog.

• Secondary Identification:"Secondary" or permanent identification cannot be removed or lost. This includes tattoos and microchips.

• File for keeping dog-related documents.
• Dog license, if applicable; secondary ID.

IDENTIFICATION

One of the most important items you should purchase for your pet is identification. Tens of thousands of pets become lost every year, and only easily-read, current identification stands between them and a permanent path away from home. Make certain your Pomeranian is well identified if you want him to get back to you, should he become lost.

ID Tags

ID tags are clipped onto collars and can be purchased in nearly all pet supply stores, some department stores, and online. Dogs should wear visible identification when at all possible.

Tattooing

Dogs are normally tattooed on the inside of the flank or groin, most often while the dog is still fairly young. The tattooed number, along with the owner's address, telephone number, and general information about the dog is registered with a national registry service or database. Tattooing is best done while the puppy is anesthetized for another veterinary procedure. However, it is not necessary for a dog to be put under general anesthesia for the process. Some breeders tattoo their puppies themselves before they are placed in new homes. Owners then have only to register their dog's information. Fees for tattooing and registration of the number are separate expenses.

Disadvantages to tattooing include the possibility that as the dog grows, the tattoo can stretch or fade until it becomes unrecognizable. Although many tattoo registration services have been combined into a central, single registry, there are still a few separate registries that do not check with other sources when a call for identification is received.

Microchipping

The use of a microchip for permanent identification reduces

some of the problems associated with tattooing. The dog does not have to be anesthetized or tolerate a procedure that can cause some stinging and discomfort during and for a short while after the process. Microchips usually last for the lifetime of a dog, and the cost of registration is included in the price of the chip in most cases. A veterinarian can inject the rice-grain-sized, biologically inactive, sealed unit under the skin between a dog's shoulders in just a few seconds. Chips, which do not contain chemicals or batteries, are then easily read via a hand-held scanner.

Even with the convenience and reliability that microchipping offers, there is uncertainty in the world of microchip scanning. Originally, manufacturers produced scanners that could only read their own system's microchips. As the technology became more popular, many scanners evolved to the point where they could detect the presence of the most commonly used microchips from other companies. In Europe, and more recently in Canada as well, new

Identification tags come in all sizes and styles these days, so your Pom can be fashionable and protected by her "jewelry."

standards have been put forth requiring that all ID chips be able to be recorded or read by all scanners, regardless of manufacturer. The transition has not been completed in the US, but some chips and scanners are currently compatible while others are not.

Regardless, microchipping is still a convenient and practical means of permanent identification. Owners choosing this ID method just need to request a chip that is going to keep up with technological changes and is currently able to be read or detected by the majority of scanners.

The safest bet for identification of your Pom is to use a dual system—ID tags and either a tattoo or microchip. Whichever you choose, be certain that you register your contact information and remember to update it if your address or phone number changes.

TRAVEL

A nice bonus about having a Pomeranian as a companion is that they are easily transported, they like to be with you wherever you are, and they travel well. Here are some tips for roaming around with your dog.

Down the Road

Poms enjoy being with you, wherever you go. If you get your dog accustomed to traveling at an early age, you can enjoy his company wherever your travels take you.

Start by getting your dog used to riding in the car to a destination other than the veterinarian's. Begin with short rides, maybe just round the block, then increase the distance, for example, a trip to a nearby park. When your Pom is comfortable with short trips, try an all day expedition before venturing out on an overnight vacation.

Coming Home

Your puppy is old enough to leave his mother, you've bought everything you can imagine to make your new companion happy, and your house is puppy-proofed and ready for your new buddy. Now it's time to go get him and bring him to his new house. To do that, you'll also need to make some preparations for the trip. It's a smart idea to take a bag of dog-related supplies with you. Try packing:

• Thermos or bottled water, water bowl, healthy treats or a small serving of what his regular food will be;

• Paper towels, carpet cleaner, sandwich bags (for solid messes), plastic bags for disposing of soiled towels or pooper scooper bags, waterless shampoo (rinse-free) for emergency cleanup if puppy gets carsick and vomits on himself, air freshener spray;

• Identification papers and tag; health and shot records, if crossing state or country borders;

• Leash and puppy collar, blanket, and chew toy for crate.

• Ask the breeder to send you home with a small supply of the food she has been feeding your puppy. And take an empty bottle, 2 liter or larger, for her to fill with the same water he has been drinking in her kennel. Switch your puppy over by mixing in your supply with some of his old, gradually increasing the quantity of the new water and food until the old is all gone. This helps reduce the chance of stomach upset.

• When planning your trip, pick routes that aren't too winding, hilly, or bumpy and which could cause your puppy to get carsick. For safety, transport the puppy in his crate. Place the crate where it will not slide or fall while the vehicle is in motion. Allow time for potty breaks. Make sure that his leash is securely fastened before you open the car doors and get him out, and exercise him in an area away from traffic.

• Ideally, travel with a family member or friend who can help you transport your new puppy. That way, when you need to stop for a break, you won't have to leave your Pom alone in the car, where he could become overheated, chilled, or anxious.

Take your dog to the veterinarian for a pre-trip check up if you're planning on being on the road for awhile. Update needed vaccinations and purchase a sufficient quantity of any medications your pet might need while he's away from home. Having a small supply of motion sickness pills from your vet might be a good idea just in case. Make copies of your dog's health and shot records to carry with you when you travel. Be prepared to locate a veterinarian if your Pom gets sick on the road, either through access to internet listings, a local phone directory, or the recommendation of a local pet supply store.

Plan and organize your trip. Find out before your arrival if pets are welcome where you want to make reservations and go sightseeing. Make a list of items to pack, including your dog's supplies. Have written instructions and permission forms for your dog's care should you be incapacitated or injured.

Keep your dog confined or restrained during travel. In an accident, a loose dog can become lost, seriously injured, or even killed. Secure a crate into a seat or cargo area (not a trunk!), and place your dog in the crate. If crating is not possible, buckle him into a pet seatbelt harness. Lift restraint seats, similar to booster seats for children, are available that allow small dogs to watch out the car window while at the same time protecting them by securing them in place.

Put home and temporary travel identification tags on your dog in case he does get away. Temporary tags should contain your cell phone number, a local phone, if applicable, and should be updated for every change in location. If your pet is micro-chipped or tattooed, keep a copy of the registration numbers with you when you're on the road. It's also a good idea to place a color photo of your pet with these papers.

Take your dog's usual food with you. Don't switch brands while traveling as this could cause digestive distress. Store food in sealed containers that prevent spoilage. Feed your dog at his usual times, using non-breakable or disposable bowls.

Don't feed or give your dog a large quantity of water one to two hours prior to travel. While en route, stop about every three

Pomeranians enjoy going everywhere with you, so accustom your dog to riding in the car from puppyhood, and he will make a great traveling companion.

hours so that your dog can relieve himself, stretch his legs and get a drink. If there is time, a small, portable exercise pen can be set up for your dog's relief and exercise needs. If you are indoors where your dog can't get to the outside, such as transfers between airplanes, carry puppy "piddle" pads with you. Your Pom can be taught to relieve himself indoors on these disposable pads. When you are outdoors, always scoop the poop! Be courteous to others and clean up after your pet. Carry sandwich bags to pick up feces and only allow your dog to relieve himself in designated pet exercise areas.

Maintain your dog's normal activity level. He'll sleep more soundly at night and be more relaxed during the day. Teach your dog traveling manners. Don't let him disturb other travelers by barking in the hotel or on a plane. Traveling with your Pom requires some extra work, but most owners feel it's worth the effort.

Should you go on a picnic or other extended trip, you can set up an exercise pen for your Pom that will keep him safe and allow him to exercise and relieve himself outside.

By Air

Air travel with your dog will require plenty of advance planning. Check with the airlines on what their pet travel policies are. Book with the one that gives you the most confidence that they can safely transport your pet, in all types of weather, in the least amount of time and with the least amount of stress (airports are noisy, confusing places).

Try to book your and your dog's reservations on a flight where he can ride on the plane with you instead of in cargo. Most Pomeranians are small enough to easily fit under the seat inside of a soft-sided carrier.

If your dog must fly in cargo, choose an airline that has a pressurized, climate controlled, and lit area specifically for pets. Use a hard crate, with clips to secure food and water bowls during the flight, and sized just big enough for your dog to stand and turn but not so large that he can get tossed around when the plane moves.

Most of the same travel rules apply for food, water, and identification. A few Poms may fly better if mildly tranquilized. Should he get nervous during the flight, just reach in and give him a reassuring pat. Before getting on a plane with your dog, have your veterinarian examine him to make certain he is healthy enough to fly.

In The Cabin

The best way for your Pom to travel by air is in the cabin with you—it's one of the great advantages of having a small dog!

LEAVING YOUR POMERANIAN

It will not always be possible to take your Pom with you when you travel. When you have to leave him behind, you can either board him in a kennel or have a petsitter come to your home. Before choosing the service or boarding facility that will take care of your dog while you're away, there are several questions you need to ask to make certain that they are reliable and capable.

Boarding

Begin your search by checking with other dog-owning friends and neighbors who travel without the company of their canine. Find out if they are happy with the kennel they use.

Does your veterinarian board pets besides for health care? Are you satisfied with their facilities and the care they normally provide for your dog? If so, then you may want to consider leaving your dog in your vet's clinic. If your vet does not board, ask them for a kennel recommendation.

Look up listings in the yellow pages. For convenience, check with the kennels that are located near your home or business first. Set up appointments to visit their facilities and meet the staff that will be caring for your dog. Ask the owner or manager for references.

When you arrive, get a tour of the kenneling and recreation areas. If a tour is refused, this may be a warning not to board your dog there. Is the facility clean, including crates, runs and yard areas? How frequently are they cleaned? How often are the dogs taken out for exercise and potty breaks? Are outside views or runs provided? Is the building safe from fire hazards? Do the dogs have access to fresh water at all times?

Does the staff truly like and understand animals, and are they attentive to them? Are they willing to accommodate your dog's special needs if he has any? Will they administer your dog's daily medication or feed the same diet given at home? Is your dog permitted to keep toys in his run?

Discuss the kennel's policies. Most require that all boarding animals be current on their vaccinations. What proof of vaccination will you need to provide? Are their rates competitive with other kennels, and do they reflect the quality of the care given? What does the kennel do in case of a medical emergency involving your dog? Is payment due before you leave or when you return? Are there standard services for which they charge extra, such as allowing them access to an exercise yard or giving medication? Get a schedule of their hours and times when you can drop off and pick up your dog.

If you must leave your Pomeranian while you go away, be sure to thoroughly research any kennels or boarding facilities before entrusting them with your friend's care.

Once you select a kennel, give them detailed, written care instructions for your dog. Leave a list of your travel itinerary, along with phone numbers where they can contact you in the event of an emergency. If permitted, send your dog's favorite chew bone and bedding to the kennel. You may want to leave one of your unlaundered shirts with your Pom—an item that has your scent and smells like home. This can comfort your dog while you're away from him and remind him you will return.

Petsitters

Some Pomeranians may be happier staying at home in familiar surroundings. If this is the best choice for your dog, you will need to find a reliable, qualified petsitter. There are two national organizations that can help you locate sitters in your area, Petsitters International and The National Association of Pet Sitters. You can also check with your dog friends to see which petsitting services they have used and would recommend.

Since a sitter will have full access to your home and be solely responsible for the care of your dog, ask for multiple references. Sitters should be fully insured and bonded. Anyone can call themselves a petsitter, but only the better ones will meet these requirements.

Before a petsitter begins her home visits, you will be asked to provide a thorough history of your Pom's habits and health status in order to provide him with the care to which he is used to receiving. It's easier for the sitter—and therefore for your dog—if you leave all of the items he needs on a daily basis (like bowls, meds, and leash) in a central location. Provide a sufficient quantity of food for more days than you plan to be gone.

Just as you would for a kennel, write down all specific care instructions, and a copy of your complete travel itinerary, including contact numbers. Furnish any information the sitter will need about your home, such as where to find the breaker panel, main water shut-off valve, and spare supplies like light bulbs or paper towels.

Rates for petsitters vary by area, but can cost about 1-1/2 times per visit what you might pay per day at a kennel. The advantages your dog gets for the extra expense may be well worth the difference. Your dog will be in familiar surroundings and able to play with his own toys and sleep in his own bed. He'll be fed his normal food at the usual times, get to walk or exercise as usual, and, if he needs medications, they can be administered just as you would give them. Although he will still be alone many hours he will receive plenty of

Petsitters

You can find petsitters in your area by visiting Petsitters International at www.petsit.com or The National Association of Petsitters at www.petsitters.org.

Another option for when you go away is to hire a pet sitter to come into your home and care for your dog.

personal attention, and the sitter can reassure your Pom that you will soon return home to him.

In-Home Boarding

Placing your Pom in a facility that specializes in boarding a limited number of small dogs in their home is another option. Although your dog is away from his home, he is still in a house with people who are there to spend at least as much time with him as you normally would. In-home boarding services match client reservations by age, size, health and temperament so that your dog is only with other dogs with whom he is compatible. Your dog will also be maintained on his normal diet and exercise routine. Prices typically range somewhere between the cost of boarding and petsitting fees.

You can find in-home boarding facilities online or in your phone directory. Schedule an appointment to see the home and meet the owners before you book your dog's visit. You may also want to take your dog to meet the owner prior to leaving him there for the first time. Ask the same questions you would of a kennel or petsitter, including references from other clients. Be prepared to leave the same detailed history and instructions as you would for other care services.

Because Pomeranians are such comfort- and home-loving dogs, in-home boarding may prove the ideal place to leave your dog when you travel.

Doggy Daycare

If you work long hours, are going to be away all day, or if your Pom needs companionship while you're out and about, consider taking him to a doggy daycare center.

Doggy daycare is a place where your dog can play, fully supervised, with other dogs suited to his temperament. There are plenty of humans around to pet him, and usually comfy beds for napping as well as toys with which he can play, and furnishings on which he can climb. Costs are usually figured per day, and tend to be slightly higher than daily rates at a kennel because of the extras, including more extensive staffing.

Facilities at daycare centers range from buildings with divided play and rest areas, to spa-like facilities complete with massages, pampered pet boutique items for sale and more. Most have outdoor exercise areas as well. Centers are well-staffed with dog-savvy personnel who have been specially trained to understand canine behavior, judge which dogs should be put together, and know if or when to intervene between dogs who may appear ready to quarrel.

Owners should choose a doggy day care center with the same care used to choose a boarding kennel. Is the ratio of staff to dogs sufficient to ensure constant supervision? Do they interact well with the dogs? Does the center contain too many dogs? Are the building and outdoor area secure and safely equipped? Do they have an arrangement with a nearby veterinarian in case your dog needs emergency treatment?

All dogs in daycare must meet minimum health requirements – vaccinations must be current, dogs must be free from internal and external parasites, as well as clear of infectious diseases. Some centers may request that your dog know and respond to basic obedience commands before accepting him as a client. Additionally, your Pom will be screened to make certain his temperament is suited to the day care environment. Overly shy, fearful or aggressive dogs are not good candidates. Since some Poms are dominant or territorial, or don't enjoy playing with strange dogs, daycare may not be the best place for them. But if your dog is friendly and outgoing with other dogs, and the center you select keeps small dogs separated from larger ones, your Pom may enjoy an outing to doggy daycare.

FEEDING
Your Pomeranian

he expression, "You are what you eat" has been touted so often that when someone hears it, they tune out any nutritional advice that might follow. But this cliché is worth heeding. For most dogs, the foundation of wellness can rest solidly on sound nutrition.

BUYING IT READY TO GO

At least a decade ago, about 95 percent of owners fed their dogs pre-prepared dog food products. In recent years that percentage has likely decreased, as owners prepare their dogs' food to better control the quality of the ingredients or provide a diet that meets specific needs. However, the majority of people still feed their dogs a product which is ready made and about which they need to understand the nutritional content.

Dry Kibble

The most popular choice of dog food on the market, kibble is crunchy bits of dry food. There are many dozens of brands available, and within these brands, manufacturers usually offer several varieties of feed. With so many choices, how is an owner supposed to figure out which food is best? By learning how to read labels and understand which ingredients are most healthy for your dog.

When dry dog food was first produced commercially and offered for sale to the general public, these products met two separate needs: to provide a convenient way for owners to feed their dogs; and to open up another market for meat packers and grain millers to sell the leftover parts from their businesses that could not be used in human foods.

As people have gained more awareness of their dogs' nutritional needs and health, manufacturers have improved the quality of ingredients in dry kibble. Ingredients that are also suitable for human consumption are offered in many products. But a word of caution— there are just as many dry foods on the market that contain discarded meats and grains as their base. Some of these components may be used to produce soybean- or corn meal, wheat mill run and rice mill, by-products, animal digest and meat by-products from an undisclosed meat source which is then utilized as a main ingredient in the kibble.

Pomeranians with food sensitivities and diet-triggered skin or hair problems may have fewer issues if these types of ingredients are avoided. In products where the whole grain or healthier parts of meat are used, the nutrients are more complete and available in a more digestible, absorbable form. Dogs who eat these foods may have better health overall.

A great deal of variation in the type of meat used can be found from one processor to another. Primary meat sources encompass beef, lamb, turkey, chicken, and even fish, as well as the by-products of these meats. Additional ingredients include the grain base which holds the kibble together, plus a wide assortment of vegetables, fruits, or herbs. Sources for these products differ as widely as do flavors.

There are also ingredients that add no nutritional value to dog food, and may actually aggravate or promote the development of certain health problems. These include sugars, salts, and artificial preservatives. When less digestible forms of grain, such as oats or bran, are used in a food, hydrochloric acid or propionic acid may be added in an attempt to make them more digestible.

Additionally, the method used to manufacture the kibble can affect the food's ability to maintain its nutritional value. The majority of dry dog food is first compounded, then pressure cooked and

To feed your Pom a high-quality kibble you need to understand what ingredients provide the nutrients.

extruded into bite-size pieces. Because the high temperatures at which the food is processed can cause vitamins and minerals to break down, following extrusion, they are sprayed onto the kibble via a fatty coating. Extrusion techniques vary by manufacturer, and affect the nutritional availability of all essential nutrients. Some dry foods are produced by baking at a lower temperature in order to preserve these nutrients. Such a process eliminates the need to apply an enriched fat since the vitamins and minerals have not been destroyed by processing.

Your puppy was probably weaned on a nutritionally sound kibble. Consult with your veterinarian or breeder before switching brands.

Before making your selection, learn to interpret the terminology on dry dog food labels, then choose the product that is healthiest for your Pomeranian. "Healthy" does not equate with "tasteless," so it is also possible to select a main meat ingredient that support's your dog's health (or any special diet he must follow because of a medical condition) while appealing to his sense of taste. If your dog is sensitive to certain foods, check the secondary ingredients, like fruits or vegetables, to make certain you are selecting a food that is safe for him.

If dry kibble is your dog food of choice, it should constitute about 70 to 90 percent of your Pom's diet. Canine nutritional experts and veterinarians usually recommend that once you select a dry food for your dog, be consistent with it. If it becomes necessary to change, do so gradually.

For a Pomeranian with allergies, feeding a single dry food may not be the best choice. Repeated exposure to the same ingredient can sensitize a dog's system so that the ingredient is seen by the body as an allergen. By rotating two or three foods, this problem can be avoided, plus finicky eaters will love the variety. Consult your veterinarian before switching your Pom's food. If he suffers from digestive disorders, a change may precipitate a flare up of symptoms, or if he is on a specific diet geared towards controlling a disease, change may not be in his best interest.

Canned

While meat of many flavors appears to be the main ingredient, canned food contains primarily water or broth—about 70- 85 percent liquid. Because of this high moisture content, it also often called soft or moist food. Vitamins, minerals, and sometimes amino acids are added to provide a balance of essential nutrients. Potatoes, vegetables, and a selection of grains such as rice or barley, and possibly even fruits such as cranberries may be blended into the mixture to hold it together or increase flavor or nutrient levels.

Synthetic preservatives are not usually added because the process of canning itself is a means of preserving the product.. Regardless, closely check the label. Some brands may still add preservatives or artificial flavor enhancers. Your dog's food will be healthier—less likely to provoke allergies or side effects, or to impact his health negatively—if it doesn't contain certain ingredients such as soy flour or soybean meal; brighteners or coloring like titanium dioxide or yellow #5; salts and sodiums like sodium alginate, chlorine chloride or sodium tripolyphosphate; and seasonings like onion powder, which may not be safe for dogs.

Most dogs enjoy the taste of canned food. For picky eaters, stirring a portion of canned food into their kibble is an excellent way to get them to eat their dry food. It's also a good method for increasing water intake for dogs who need higher amounts of liquid in their diets.

In Pomeranians who have developed dental problems, feeding canned food can either prove beneficial or harmful. If your dog's teeth are prone to decay, dry food will help keep his teeth cleaner. However if your dog has misaligned or missing teeth, canned food may cause him less discomfort while eating. In general, canned food can make up to around 20 to 25 percent of your dog's healthy diet.

When choosing a canned food, be careful to select a brand that utilizes a high quality meat source, similar to human grade meats, and one to which

For picky eaters, it's helpful to mix a small amount of quality canned dog food in with their kibble to improve palatability.

your dog is not sensitive. Avoid products that use a low grade of meat, or sugars, salts, and other unnecessary additives. Since canned food tends to be higher in calories, don't give your dog too much, regardless of how much he likes it—a little serving goes a long way.

Semi-Moist

Designed to resemble hamburger patties or chunks of roast beef, these foods are marketed to appeal to people. Few dogs will take notice of their appearance. Semi-moist foods have a long shelf life and are conveniently packaged. So what's not to like? The payload of sugars and artificial preservatives, colors, and flavors they deliver with each serving. Propylene glycol, a main additive in some semi-moist foods or treats, is a gooey, mostly tasteless liquid used in the manufacturing of de-icing agents and polyester compounds, and as a solvent for paints and plastics. The Food and Drug Administration (FDA) has placed propylene glycol on its "generally recognized as safe" (GRAS) list and permits its use in food, where it is utilized to retain moisture and as a dissolving agent for flavoring and coloring.

Although it is on the GRAS list, propylene glycol is also listed in the database of the Agency for Toxic Substances and Disease Registry (ATSDR), a branch of the Center for Disease Control (CDC). According to the ATSDR, propylene glycol can increase the amount of acid in the body, which in sufficient quantities could cause metabolic problems.

Semi-moist food can be a source of hidden sodium and is high in sugars in the form of sucrose, corn syrup, and fructose. With their propensity to hypoglycemia (see more on low blood sugar in Chapter 8), it is wise not to feed Pomeranians foods that are high in simple carbohydrates, which quickly convert to sugar. Although sugary foods will temporarily raise blood sugar to more normal levels, the long-term result is an actual drop in glucose, causing a hypoglycemic state. Furthermore, sugars tend to promote tooth decay, another problem for Poms.

Buying Balanced

Commercial dog foods should all meet a minimum nutritional requirement. The Association of American Feed Control Officials (AAFCO) is an organization that analyzes companion animal food and its ingredients for proper nutrient levels and ratios. Formal approval by AAFCO is usually received before a manufacturer can claim that his dog food products are complete and balanced. Most manufacturers perform palatability studies, along with nutritional analyses, to determine if the ingredients are digestible and absorbable (as energy and nutrients) in the food's final form.

When shopping for dog food, look for a product that has been approved by AAFCO. Keep in mind that the AAFCO stamp of approval does not necessarily equate with being the best choice for your Pom. The organization does not recognize the nutritional need for all nutrients, some of which may be important to canine health. This exclusion includes omega 3, an essential fatty acid that must be fed in proper ratio with omega 6 in order to maintain good fur and skin condition.

DOG FOOD DECONSTRUCTED

One of the smartest actions you can take for your Pom is to carefully read the ingredient label before buying a dog food product. But don't stop there. Learn what each ingredient is, what the source for those ingredients might be, and any possible long-term health effects from consuming some of the following substances on a daily basis.

The FDA's Center for Veterinary Medicine determines the guidelines for how an ingredient is defined, and the AAFCO dictates what the use of ingredients shall mean as listed on a dog food label. If you're uncertain what an alphabet-soup of an ingredient name is or means, call or e-mail the manufacturer; most dog food products have contact information provided on their label.

Additives

Substances are added to food during processing to preserve, color, flavor, or stabilize the ingredients. Nutrients may also be considered additives if they do not naturally occur in a food product and are added during processing to make a food nutritious.

Animal Digest

This refers to the material that remains after a process of cleaning, boiling, and separating, sometimes with chemical enzymes, the unused portions of an animal used as a meat source in dog food. Digest is to exclude hair, horns, hooves, teeth, and feathers.

Artificial

A description meaning "manufactured"; a substance that does not occur naturally.

Beet Pulp

The residue remaining in dried sugar beets after the sugar portion is removed and dried. It is an insoluble fiber and is moderately fermentable. Usually added to dog food for the purpose of "compacting stool" for easier owner clean up. Beet pulp may serve to provide necessary fiber and promote the growth of beneficial

Your Pom's energy level and overall vitality comes from the nutrients that are in the food he eats.

intestinal bacteria. But in some dogs, it can cause the cells that absorb and breakdown nutrients to function improperly or fail, depriving the dog's body of necessary nutrients and allowing bacterial overgrowth. In the light-colored Pomeranian, beet pulp may have some undetermined relationship to problems with tear staining.

By-Products

The unprocessed parts of animals remaining after the muscle meat has been removed for use. It can include blood, bone, brains, intestines (emptied), kidneys, livers, lungs, spleen, stomach, and some fatty tissues. It should exclude hair, hooves, horn, and teeth.

By-Product Meal

By-product meal is made by rendering the processed parts. It should exclude the same items as above, plus manure, contents of the digestive tract, and pieces of hide. Poultry by-product meal may include the use of feet, intestines, necks, and undeveloped eggs but excludes feathers and heads.

BHA and BHT

Butylated hydroxyanisole (BHA) and butylated hydrozytuolene (BHT) are used as preservatives of fats and grains as found in dog food. According to profiles done by the National Institutes of Health, they are suspected carcinogens, as tests of mice and rats fed BHA and BHT resulted in the formation of various types of malignancies in portions of the digestive tract. The use of BHT is reported to be prohibited in the manufacture of pet foods in Europe.

Grains

The cereal and other grains used in the production of dog food can include rice, wheat, barley, oats, corn, soy, and others. Dogs with allergies may have fewer problems if they are not fed foods with soy, corn, or wheat grains.

Grains may be ground or whole and are usually noted as such. Grain parts include the bran, hulls (the coarse outer coverings), germ, and germ meal (the inner part of the grain kernel normally processed to remove the oil). Grain meal, especially soybean meal, may be processed mechanically, but it may also be dehulled using chemical solvents.

Gums

Usually used as thickeners to give the "creamy" feel of fat, gum sources vary and can include complex carbohydrates from plants or even microorganisms similar to yeast. Xanthan gum comes from the microorganism that causes the slimy black rot that sometimes grows on broccoli or cauliflower.

Meat

Is designated to mean the skeletal muscle tissue, and tongue, heart, esophagus, or diaphragm of animals such as cattle, chicken, turkey, or lamb. It may or may not include skin, sinew, or blood vessels which can be found in these tissues. It is to exclude feet, hair, heads, entrails, feathers, and such. **Meat meal and bone meal** is the processed product derived from meat parts and also includes processed bone.

Middling, Mill Run

The "in-between" leftover parts after processing the bran, hulls, or germ, mill runs are usually bits of all parts and also include "tail of the mill," the grain debris that is collected after several days' processing and sold for feed production.

Natural

A term referring to a substance derived from an organic (animal or vegetable) origin as opposed to manufactured chemicals; a food product containing no chemical additives.

Knowing what's in your Pom's food can assure you you're giving him what he needs to grow strong and healthy.

Premium

A presumably higher standard of quality for the ingredients and nutrition in dog foods.

Organic

Refers to substances derived from living organisms. It may also indicate that the ingredient was produced from a plant or animal source where no chemicals were used, such as pesticides, growth hormones, and so forth.

Preservative

A chemical substance that prevents decomposition or fermentation in food; may be natural or artificial.

Titanium Dioxide

A white powder normally used in toothpaste and cosmetics as a brightener or color enhancer. It may be used in dog foods, along with artificial color, to make a product more visually appealing to an owner.

Quality Counts

Prices for pet foods are as varied as the choices offered. Like any other item that consumers purchase, normally the price is determined by the quality of the item and the cost of the effort required to produce that level of quality.

In recent years, stories have been posted on the internet and circulated through e-mail lists about the horrifying, indescribable "things" which are put into pet food. Some of these stories are urban myths, others are exaggerations, and sadly some are true. This is why it is important that you understand what the sources are for the ingredients when choosing a dog food.

When an animal is slaughtered for human consumption, a large portion of the carcass and organs remain. These remnants are often what is used as the meat source in pet food. Since dogs in the wild would normally eat these parts, using them to produce dog food is not necessarily a bad practice. What is necessary is to ascertain that a sufficient quantity of vitamins and protein are available from these sources.

The time to worry about the meat source is when "4D" animals are used. "4-D" animals are those recognized by the FDA and USDAA as "down/disabled, diseased, dying, or dead," and they are not allowed to be sold for human consumption. Although the process of rendering this type of meat kills most disease-causing bacteria, it does not remove the toxins generated by the bacteria. These toxins can cause disease in dogs. Conditions that caused the animal to be 4D are numerous and often the diseased tissue is processed into the food product.

Worst of all, it is possible that some dog foods may include undefined meat sources—meats that are derived from rendering the remains of dogs and cats euthanized in animal pounds. There is no prohibition against the sale of these animal remains to rendering plants, and they are offered for re-sale to any off-brand pet food manufacturer who wishes to buy them. Several years ago, an investigative story in the **San Francisco Chronicle** disclosed this hidden practice, and the FDA and American Veterinary Medical

True Health

"True health can't be maintained by feeding garbage," explains veterinary practitioner Shawn Messonnier, DVM, author of The Natural Health Bible for Dogs & Cats, and columnist of The Holistic Pet. "Some ingredients can increase inflammation in the body. Since many diseases have inflammation as a cause or contributing factor, feeding the best foods is imperative to good health. A healthy diet is the foundation of everything I recommend."

Association confirmed it to be true.

Ingredient labels will not mention the inclusion of 4D or domestic animals, so how do you know if the dog food might contain these items? The price will be very low, and the product may contain mostly animal digest, meat by-products, and meat meal, without including the type of animal (such as chicken, lamb, etc.) from which the meat was derived. It may also have a strong or unappealing odor that is often masked by fatty sprays designed to make the kibble taste better.

The fats with which dry food is usually sprayed may be another ingredient where the source of origin is a potential problem. Since there are no regulations against the practice, some manufacturers may buy the leftover, used grease from restaurants and the food preparation industry. Again, this will not be noted on the label, but can be suspected if the fat sources have lengthy, indecipherable names, and if the price on the food is cheap.

The bottom line on pet food pricing: if it's bargain basement priced, the food is not a good deal for your dog. But beware of the opposite side of this coin. Just because a dog food carries a hefty price tag, does not guarantee that it will be an exceptionally

If you won't read the ingredient labels on your Pom's food, he may have to stop reading the newspaper and do it for you.

nutritious, healthy, or flavorful food for your dog. Before making a final decision, read consumer reviews and ask other Pomeranian owners for recommendations of brands on which their dogs have thrived. You will pay more for premium grade foods, but in the long run your dog will reap the benefits in improved nutrition and better health.

MAKING IT YOURSELF

Another dietary option is to forgo commercial dog foods and prepare your Pom's food yourself. Home prepared and raw diets have become increasingly popular, and with a little research about nutrition, some time and effort, you can give your Pom a healthy diet lovingly made in your own kitchen.

Home Prepared Dog Foods

To follow the trend for healthier eating, some owners are now preparing their dogs' food at home instead of buying it. There are several reasons to do this: to give you the satisfaction of making your dog feel special; to supply higher quality, human grade foods that you purchase; and to meet the needs of a special diet or avoid problem ingredients.

Preparing your Pom's food can be as simple as increasing the amount of healthy meals you prepare for the rest of your family, and giving it to your dog. Or it can be as elaborate as buying dog-friendly cook books, special ingredients, and making multiple daily dishes just for your dog.

Before embarking on a canine culinary venture, it is important to learn all that you can about nutrition for your dog. Read books that offer not only recipes, but a nutritional analysis of the recipes as well as information on basic canine nutrition. If you prefer to concoct your own special blends of dog food, consider consulting a veterinary nutritionist about the content and quantity you plan to feed.

Understand your dog's individual health concerns, in addition

Nutritional Terms

- **Amino acids:** The organic building blocks for protein; the "essential amino acids" cannot be made by the body and must be obtained from the diet.

- **Balanced:** When nutrients occur in the proper ratio to one another, the food is said to be balanced.

- **Calorie, Kcal:** A unit of heat used to express the energy value of food. This information is used to determine feeding directions. Dog food is calculated by "kcals," kilocalories of metabolizable energy per kilogram of food.

- **Carbohydrate:** Starches and sugars that are broken down and quickly utilized as a source of ready energy; may also include fiber. Carbs are either simple, those which breakdown more easily and are more rapidly absorbed, or complex, those which require more digestive processes to breakdown, and which take slightly longer to be absorbed.

- **Chelated minerals:** Minerals structurally changed by a chemical process into a more digestible form for better absorption.

- **Chemical:** A substance composed of various processed chemicals; chemicals occur naturally or may be manufactured

- **Complete:** When a food contains the nutrients essential to maintain life and basic health, it is said to be complete.

- **Enriched:** When a food has vitamins and minerals added after cooking or processing, it is said to be enriched.

- **Essential:** Necessary, indispensable, required to maintain life.

Your Pom's skin and coat are indicators of the quality of his diet. If they are both looking and feeling good, he is probably eating well.

to knowing what appeals to his tastebuds, before selecting the ingredients for his homemade meals. Most of the time, low-sodium/salt, no or low sugars, and avoiding excess fats are the best choices. Protein in the form of meat, eggs, or possibly dairy products should constitute between 10 and 30 percent of your dog's diet, complex carbohydrates, including fiber and whole grains, about 25 to 45 percent, and fat, an essential nutrient, the remainder.

Any fresh, lean cut which your Pomeranian likes can serve as the meat source. Possible choices are lamb, chicken, turkey, fish, venison, sometimes beef, and organ meats like liver, kidneys, or brain. The fat in the meat source may be sufficient so that no additional is required. If it is necessary to add fat, use oils like olive or sunflower, but stay away from corn or soy oils since they may be linked to causing or aggravating some health problems.

Carbohydrates can come from whole grains such as rice, oats, barley, and possibly wheat, if your dog is not sensitive to this grain. A nearly limitless assortment of vegetables and fruits should be included to provide complex carbohydrates. Avoid onions, raisins, grapes, and some nuts like almonds and macadamia, which are purported to induce serious reactions in some dogs. You may also wish to exclude veggies like cabbage that can ferment and cause flatulence.

Herbs commonly used to flavor your own dishes may also be used in your dog's recipes, but use sparingly. And offer your Pomeranian a changing selection of foods. Unlike the recommendation to always feed a single dry dog food, homemade doggy meals can and should rotate their ingredients, unless you have been instructed otherwise by your veterinarian.

Cook your dog's meals with the same precautions you use when handling ingredients for human consumption. Store unused portions in the refrigerator and discard any that remains uneaten after about three days.

Check in a few weeks to see how your dog's skin and coat look. Is the skin supple and without flakes? Is his fur shiny and full? Does your dog appear more energetic or act like he feels better? If yes, then you are likely on the right track with his menus. Regardless, remember to keep your veterinarian informed and up to date on your Pom's health when you feed a home cooked diet.

Raw Diets

The ultimate choice in home-prepared dog food is feeding raw. Sometimes referred to as BARF, which stands for Biologically Appropriate Raw Foods, this special diet is meant to closely replicate the foods that a dog might eat in the wild. The theory behind feeding this primal fare is that this food form is what a dog's system was made to digest, and thus provides nutrition that results in the greatest levels of health.

Raw meal recipes are based on combining about 60 to 70 percent raw meat and about 30 to 40 percent vegetables, preferably fresh. Meats used are usually chicken, beef, or lamb, obtained fresh from a butcher and prepared by home chunking or grinding on the day of preparation. Vegetables can be whatever your dog likes and are ground in with the meat. Carbohydrates in the form of cereal grains like barley, oats, rice, or even pasta can be added, as can some fruits. Bones are normally included in the BARF diet, also in raw form. With the proper nutrient balance, raw can be fed either a few times a week, or for all meals.

Safety

The thought of feeding raw may make some owners' stomachs turn and can definitely raise questions of safety and health. Raw meat harbors greater numbers of disease-inducing bacteria than does cooked meat. But dogs have shorter intestinal tracts and more acidic stomachs, and may be less likely to be affected adversely by E. coli or salmonella, the bacterial culprits that most commonly cause food poisoning.

Feeding raw requires that the meat source be fresh and clean, and that is it safely handled and processed. Some sources suggest freezing the meat before preparing the meals (thaw only in the refrigerator, never at room temperature), and others suggest a quick dip in boiling water, or a rinse with grapefruit seed extract to reduce or kill bacteria. Once

Making the Switch to Homemade

Homemade dog food can be used as a supplement to dry kibble or as your dog's entire diet. When you switch your dog to meals that are entirely home cooked, do so gradually to avoid digestive upset. Observe him for any signs of digestive distress or other problems that might arise due to the change. Are his bowel and bladder habits normal? Does his urine and stool look the same or even better than they normally do? Does your dog have flatulence? Is he vomiting or eating grass? Is he lethargic or has his appetite decreased? If so, these could be signs that his home prepared menu needs changed.

Foods to Avoid

Avoid giving your Pom:

- cooked bones which may splinter
- alcoholic beverages
- chocolate
- coffee or tea
- grapes or raisins
- onions
- almonds or macadamia nuts
- scraps or leftovers you wouldn't eat
- fatty, greasy foods

prepared, raw meals need to be separated into individual serving size portions, packaged and sealed, then frozen. Just like meats for human consumption, shelf life is limited, even in the freezer, so date the package before storing and discard it if it becomes too old. Prepared raw meat meals should be thawed in the refrigerator where they should never be stored longer than two days.

There is also a risk to feeding bones. Although uncooked bones are softer and less likely to splinter, the possibility still exists for bone fragments to become lodged in or perforate the mouth, esophagus, stomach, or intestines. Such obstructions or perforations require medical attention, often emergency surgery, and can result in death. Because of the Pom's tiny size, if you are going to feed raw bones, they should be completely ground in with the meat and vegetable mixture.

Preparation

Preparing a raw diet for your Pom's meals can be a rather complicated process that involves frequent shopping trips for ingredients, and the purchase of supplies such as grinders, knives, cutting boards, and storage containers for making and packaging the meals. Extensive precautions must be taken when handling the raw meat and the implements used on it. Then when the preparation is complete, a thorough cleaning and sanitation of the prep items and surfaces must follow. Several dog food manufacturers offer a foundation product meant to provide a complete and balanced raw diet, and which helps reduce the amount of effort needed to prepare raw. These products come frozen, and owners add a few ingredients of their own choosing after thawing.

Feeding raw meat can pose serious health risks to both animals and humans. Gastroenteritis, amoebic intestinal infection, nausea, vomiting, diarrhea, dehydration, and even death can ensue if the raw meat is contaminated with enough bacteria. Dogs can become carriers of some bacterial gastrointestinal disease without being infected, posing a risk to other animals and humans in the household. If you're going to feed a raw diet to your dog, be extremely cautious in your purchases and preparations, and remain alert for any symptoms of gastrointestinal illness. For more information about safety cautions regarding raw diets for animals, visit the FDA's site at www.fda.gov/cvm/guidance/Guide122.doc.

Despite the involved preparation, BARF diets may be a route to optimum health. Some owners swear by a raw diet for dogs who have certain skin, coat, thyroid, or intestinal problems. Before starting your dog on a BARF diet, always consult with your veterinarian and contact her immediately if your dog shows symptoms of a new illness.

TIME FOR DINNER

For optimum nutrition, dogs need to be fed regular meals, usually within a certain time frame. But a little flexibility in feeding schedules is also acceptable. A dog that can adapt to small changes in his meal times will be less stressed when you are delayed in getting his food in front of him by life's unavoidable, unpredictable events.

Making the Switch to Raw

When changing your dog to a raw diet, make the switch gradually over a period of at least 7 to 10 days, beginning with small portions served into his regular food. Just as with any other dietary change, monitor your dog's health closely during the trial period to determine if raw is best for him. With the proper nutrient balance, raw can be fed either a few times a week or for all meals.

How often and how much you feed your dog depends largely on his age, health status, and activity level. Pomeranian owners should keep in mind that this is an active breed. Despite their diminutive stature, they still have the same, and sometimes higher, nutritional requirements as that of larger dogs. Because of his small size, it may be more difficult for a Pom to ingest enough calories or nutrients in one or even two daily feedings. So, unless your Pom is a couch potato, choose a food that is energy- and nutrient-dense to help maximize the nutrition he receives from the small portion it will take to fill him up at meal time.

Feeding Puppies

Puppies need to eat at frequent intervals. They need to consume more calories because of their increased energy levels, and they require higher levels of nutrients to support their growing bodies.

Until age 3 to 4 months, puppies usually need to eat at least four times daily. Between the ages of 5 and 8-10 months, three daily feedings may be sufficient. After the age of 1 year, when they have reached full growth, they can be placed on an adult feeding schedule (see below).

Space meals about 3 to 4 hours apart over a period of 13 to 16 hours while your puppy is on a four-times-daily schedule. Serve the first meal when you and pup wake up, and the last about an hour or so before he goes to bed. Three meals should be evenly spaced throughout the day from waking until bedtime.

Use the same guidelines for choosing a puppy food as you would any other dog food. It's best to bring home a bit of your breeder's kibble to continue feeding your puppy as he adapts to his new home. If you plan on changing brands, do so gradually, taking at least three or more days. Mix in a little of the new food with the old, until you are no longer serving the original food.

Puppies can usually be switched to an adult kibble by the time they are nearing one year of age. Additionally, several brands of premium dog food fill their kibble with sufficient, quality nutrients that they do not offer a separate puppy formula. Because these foods have the right nutrients in proper ratio and quantity, the additional daily feedings your puppy receives provide the extra calories and minerals necessary to support his growth. Choose the type which best helps your puppy to thrive.

Feeding Adult Dogs

Although not fully grown or mature, by the age of 7 to 9 months, as far as diet is concerned, your Pomeranian can be considered an adult and is ready to be fed regular food. He won't completely reach adulthood until sometime between the ages of 18 to 24 months, but once he has left the rapid growth stage of early puppyhood, puppy food is too rich and too high in some nutrients such as calcium to continue feeding.

It used to be suggested that adult dogs should be fed once daily, but following the results of studies, this

More Nutritional Terms

Fat: A source of food energy, found in both plants and animals, that is absorbed moderately quickly. There are many different fats.

Fatty Acids (FA): A sub-component of fat. Some FAs, known as the "essential fatty acids," cannot by synthesized in the body and must be obtained in the diet; examples are Omega-6, Omega-3, and linoleic; both the amount and ratio of FAs consumed are nutritionally important to skin and fur.

Fiber: A form of partially or wholly indigestible carbohydrates found in plants. Fiber can be fermentable or non-fermentable. Fermentable fiber is broken down into some fatty acids; non-fermentable fiber provides bulk; a moderately fermentable fiber helps maintain fluid content and movement of the stool through the intestines.

Metabolism: The workings of the physical and chemical processes in the body, especially related to digestion and utilization of nutrients. It is the process by which energy is made available to the body.

Minerals: Non-organic substances that are components of the skeletal structure, and are essential for normal nerve conduction and fluid balance in the body.

Nutrient: A nourishing substance that must be provided by food, or as a component of food, since it cannot by synthesized by the body. Essential nutrients include proteins, carbohydrates, fat, vitamins, and minerals, and are necessary for growth and to maintain normal, life functions.

Nutrition: The process of absorbing and utilizing nutrients, in a manner that promotes wellness and supports the body and its functions.

Obesity: Increase in body weight, caused by the storage of excess fat, that exceeds physical requirements.

Protein: Composed of amino acids, proteins are the basic elements that comprise the essential material of all cells. They are the building blocks of the body, used for muscles, organs, enzymes, hormones, and immune system. Protein is the least readily available form of energy, and is used primarily for building and maintaining the body.

Supplement: A separate product from food; used to add a nutrient that is perceived to be missing from the diet.

Vitamins: Organic substances found in food. Vitamins are an essential component of nutrition. They are necessary in small amounts for normal metabolic processes; however they do not provide energy nor are they materials used in the building of cells.

thinking has changed. Because of their more rapid metabolisms and their small stomachs, Poms may not be able to get enough energy and nutrients from a single feeding. And a single daily feeding may lead to problems with hypoglycemia, a too-common problem for this small dog, anyway.

How Often?

Most dogs, including Pomeranians, feel better if they are fed twice daily throughout their adult life. If your Pom is hypoglycemic, three meals a day may be more suitable. Meal times for adults should be spaced evenly apart, about every 12 hours, once in the morning and once in the evening. If your schedule permits, a third meal, should be fed in between. If this is not possible, try to feed your Pom at lunch time, or as soon as you come home from work.

Pomeranians will do best if fed at the same time each day, preferably twice daily.

Feeding Seniors

As dogs age, their metabolisms slow and energy levels drop. Older dogs may develop a tendency to gain weight, while it is also possible for some older dogs to become too thin. These changes in weight depend largely on your dog's overall health status and activity level.

The age at which this happens varies from dog to dog. Generally, dogs are considered senior at age seven, but for the longer-lived Pomeranian, senior status may be a few more years away. It may prove difficult to determine exactly which day you should change your dog's food to a senior product, so watch for subtle clues that he's slowing down.

Some of the best clues as to when it's time to switch to a senior food can be gleaned from results of blood tests taken at an annual well-dog exam. Indicators of kidney, heart, liver, and digestive tract function are the signs that will say when, and what type of senior food your Pomeranian may need.

For those prone to weight gain, a food with reduced fats and calories may be the right recipe. Seniors that are underweight, or dogs whose finicky eating habits have increased with age, will need

more calories and possibly more protein. Recent studies have shown that aging dogs need more protein to maintain muscle mass and normal organ function. Only in specific health conditions, such as when the kidneys fail to process protein correctly, is it necessary to reduce an aging dog's protein consumption.

As your Pomeranian grows older, watch closely for changes in eating habits that may indicate the beginning of an age-related health problem with the liver, pancreas, heart, or other aging organs. Special diets may be needed to compensate for failing health. Ask your veterinarian which is best for your senior.

An older dog may lose some sense of taste and smell which can make food less appealing. Adding flavorful but healthy tidbits of meat, sodium-free broth, canned food, or soft vegetables may pique interest in a failing appetite. A healthy and tasty diet is one of the best ways you can show your senior Pom that you still care.

Free-Choice Feeding

Leaving dry food in a bowl that is available for your dog all through the day—and maybe night too—is a meal plan known as free-choice feeding. This option allows the tiny Pom who may eat slowly, or a senior who may only eat a little at a time, to be able to nibble when he pleases. It can be a useful alternative for finicky eaters who can't be persuaded to eat an entire meal at a scheduled time. And for the energetic, hypoglycemic Pom (see Chapter 8 for more information), it may be the only choice for maintaining normal blood sugar levels.

Many breeders recommend using free-choice feeding for puppies to prevent hypoglycemia and provide enough energy for toy dogs who may not be able to ingest enough calories at one meal to maintain them until the next scheduled feeding time. When a puppy reaches about six months, then again every couple of months into adulthood, he can be evaluated for weight gain: if his weight stays satisfactory, then he can be kept on a free-choice feeding plan.

Free-choice feeding should not be used for Pomeranians who show an inclination to overeat or gain weight. For households with multiple dogs, free-choice feeding may not work as well because it becomes quite difficult to monitor individual food intake. Besides the possibility of a fight over food breaking out, some dogs may eat too much food while others eat too little, and special diets can't be controlled.

Do the best you can to stick with a routine when it comes to feeding.

SPECIAL DIETS

If your dog develops a health condition like diabetes, inflammatory bowel, kidney, or heart disease, he may need to be placed on a controlled diet consisting of a special prescription food. A few pet food manufacturers supply a large variety of canned and some dry foods made from ingredients aimed directly at preventing some conditions, controlling symptoms of others, or restricting and balancing specific nutrients in the diet. These foods are available only by prescription and must be purchased through a veterinary clinic.

Dogs who need these special foods will first have been tested for and diagnosed with a specific condition by a veterinarian. The appropriate food is prescribed and a diet planned out as part of the treatment plan. These foods may need to be fed for only a limited period of time, or for the life of your dog. They may be given once or twice daily, either as the sole item in the diet or in conjunction with other regulated foods. Your vet will also advise you about what foods your dog may have and those which he must not be fed while he is eating these specially formulated and balanced foods.

Before taking your dog off of a prescription diet, check with your veterinarian.

Even on a special diet, it may be possible for you to offer your dog treats or some home cooked meals, as long as you know which ingredients and nutrients to use, withhold, or limit. In some cases, preparing your dog's food may be the special diet that is just right for managing his health.

How Much to Feed

With such a wide range of weights existing in Poms, how much to feed will depend entirely on your dog's size, activity level, health condition, and feeding schedule. The quantity of dry food given per day can range anywhere from barely 1/2 cup to almost 2 cups. Canned food, home prepared supplementary food, and treats need to be figured into the total amount of food (and calories!) fed daily.

In general, puppies may need more food than adults, but don't overfeed them, either. Adults dogs will eat slightly less than growing pups. But dogs that are active showing, competing, or even doing frequent therapy visits will also need more food or a food with more calories, and higher protein and fat content.

The amount a senior dog is fed should not change drastically, possibly a little more or a little less than his adult diet. And you should still feed at the same times as usual. With a few dogs, a third meal may need to be added back into the schedule, but this should be done on the advice of your vet.

Be guided by your dog's weight and activity level when determining how much kibble to scoop into his bowl at all stages of life.

Elimination Diets

Special diets may also include elimination diets for dogs who have food-related allergies or digestive dysfunction. On an elimination diet, your dog will be restricted to a single, "novel" protein and carbohydrate source. "Novel" means that your dog would never have eaten the ingredient before. Such uncommon proteins can include buffalo, duck, venison, fish, and kangaroo. Because cereal grains are often allergens, novel carbohydrates used in elimination diets are usually starchy vegetables like potatoes, sweet potatoes, yams, or peas.

While on an elimination diet, treats, edible chew toys, or rawhide-type toys are completely prohibited. The test diet usually lasts anywhere from four to eight weeks, but a trend for improvement or a lack of change may be noticeable within two weeks.

Once the trial is ended, a new food may be introduced, and can be maintained as long as no signs of allergies or digestive dysfunction occur. If symptoms return, the elimination diet should be started again. Then your dog can either be switched to yet a different food at the end, or maintained on the hypoallergenic diet.

Dogs being fed prescription or elimination diets should be closely observed for changes in their health and nutritional status, as well as bladder and bowel habits. If there are problems or if you have questions, contact your veterinarian at once.

SUPPLEMENTS

Any nutrient like vitamins, minerals, amino acids, cultures, enzymes, and derivatives or complex compounds of these substances, can be considered as supplements when they are added to a diet. They are concentrated, isolated versions of nutrients or ingredients that can be found in various food or organic sources.

In most cases, dogs who are fed a premium-quality kibble as the mainstay of their diet are more than likely receiving the proper amount of vitamins and minerals in the correct ratios. Supplementing these nutrients is seldom necessary in such diets.

Actually, some health problems are attributable to over supplementation. Fat-soluble vitamins, like A, can cause liver toxicity in high doses. Potassium out of balance with magnesium can result in muscle cramps, heart rhythm irregularities, and digestive upset. Minerals like calcium can contribute to kidney and heart problems, and skeletal malformation.

If you are feeding a diet which requires that you add multiple supplements on a regular basis, this is a strong indication that the food is not meeting your dog's nutritional needs. Look for different ingredients, or another brand—one that provides all the essential nutrients without having to add additional products.

However, some situations may warrant the addition of certain supplements to your dog's diet. Your veterinarian might advise you to provide additional vitamins and minerals if your dog is recovering from surgery, serious illness, or an injury, where a temporary increase in these nutrients may facilitate healing. Supplements such as glucosamine and chondroitin may help support joint health in arthritis or patellar luxation. Fatty-acid supplements, such as fish oils, evening primrose, and flax seed oils, may prove beneficial to Pomeranians with conditions that have a negative impact on skin or fur.

If your veterinarian identifies a particular food allergy your Pom has, he can help you find a special elimination diet to avoid that ingredient.

Because nutritious food is a cornerstone to good health, a proper diet, along with nutritional supplements, may help prevent or relieve symptoms in Pomeranians prone to various health problems. Before adding any supplements to your dog's diet regimen, consult with your veterinarian about which ones to use, how much you should give, and for how long your dog should receive the supplement.

TREATS

The snacks—"junk food"—of the doggy world, treats are probably available in as many flavors, shapes, and sizes as there are types of dogs. Because treats are not designed to be a component of a dog's regular diet, they are not made with nutrition in mind. They are meant to appeal to doggy taste buds—and to owners' hearts when they make their dogs happy by feeding them treats.

Treats are made with the same variety of ingredients and additives that are used in dry kibble and semi-moist foods. But they tend to have more artificial flavorings and color added, and are usually higher in fat, sugars, sodium, and calories. Because of this, a slight reduction in quantity of main food should be made in your dog's diet to allow for the additional caloric intake if you are feeding him treats (and what dog owner is not going to give their Pomeranian the occasional tasty tidbit?).

For the Pomeranian who has food sensitivities or is on a special diet for a health condition like kidney disease, treats must be selected with the same care as when choosing his daily food. In these circumstances, it is best to consult with your veterinarian about what brands or types of treats you can offer and how often.

Your Pom should never be away from cool, clean water for long periods. Be sure to have some available when you're traveling or working with your dog.

It is possible to buy healthy, lower calorie, more "natural" treats. Dry treats are preferable over moist ones because they are better for teeth and may contain less artificial additives. Just read labels closely when selecting a healthy treat for your dog. Or offer him a baby carrot, a bite of broccoli, or a couple of blueberries.

If you are eating a healthy meal yourself, it's not unreasonable to give your dog a bite of your plain baked yam or a nibble of your lean chicken as a treat. But put these tidbits in his bowl instead of feeding them directly from your plate; this helps discourage begging. Owners who want to go the extra step, or whose dogs are on restricted diets, can prepare treats from scratch. Just don't go overboard. Follow the same guidelines that apply to preparing a healthy home-cooked diet for your dog.

BATTLE OF THE BULGE

Nearly every week there's at least one story in the news about obesity. Reports consistently show that more people are gaining more and more weight. The news is no different in the world of pets—more dogs are getting heavier and suffering the consequences of excess weight than ever before.

Like their larger Nordic cousins, most Pomeranians like to eat. And like all northern breeds, the weight can pile on quickly. This is because the metabolism of the Nordic breeds is geared to see them through tough winters that may be short on food. The dogs' ancestors were programmed to eat as much as they could when food was available, and their bodies would store the calories as fat. Then, in lean times, they could break down the fat into energy and survive with less food. Although many years have passed and plenty of food is readily available to today's Pomeranians, their metabolism still retains its ancient programming.

Even after eating a full meal, your Pom may try to convince you that he is still hungry and needs more food. But don't let those cute dark eyes and his pitiful looks cajole you into giving him too much to eat. Plus, just as in the selection of people foods, there is a huge variety of tasty dog foods and treats, that make it too easy for a dog to pack on the pounds while happily chowing down.

Water

People who are conscious of chemical contaminants in their tap water may install a home water filtration system or use bottled water for their personal drinking source. Bottled water has usually been specially filtered and "cleaned" before being bottled. Offering this water to your dog is perfectly acceptable.

Besides processed drinking water, other bottled waters available include natural spring water and distilled water. Distilled water is processed so that all mineral content is removed. It is not intended to be used as drinking water as it does not contain the nutrients necessary for proper adsorption of fluid. Spring water usually is bottled at a ground source and may be filtered to remove impurities. Serving spring water is also a viable option for your Pomeranian.

If you have a light colored Pomeranian whose fur tends to stain around the mouth, you may want to avoid offering him tap water to drink. Ingredients like chlorine and fluoride, added to most municipally treated water supplies, may increase the tendency for fur to discolor. Well water that is high in iron, sulfur, or other minerals containing naturally occurring chemicals with color, can also result in staining.

Whatever type of water you choose to provide for your dog, be certain that he always has access to a clean bowl filled with fresh water.

It is not a dog's fault if he gets too hefty, since he is not the one determining what he is eating each day. The responsibility for obesity in a dog can be laid directly at the feet of his owner. What's the best way to address the problem of obesity? Prevent it by not overfeeding your dog.

This may not always be possible. Weight is easily gained while a dog is inactive or recuperating from surgery such as patellar repair, a common problem in Pomeranians. Or if you have just adopted an older dog, he may come into your home already overweight. And

Choose the treats you give your Pom as carefully as the food you serve him.

when your dog stares at you as if he's going to faint from hunger, you may not always be able to resist his demand for a tasty tidbit.

The urge to express your affection and love for your Pom with food must be resisted. Food is not love. Love means keeping your dog at a healthy weight. Just because you feel guilty when he stares at you while you're snacking, doesn't mean you should give your dog some of your sugar cookies or potato chips. The real guilt should come only if you consistently overfeed your dog and allow him to gain too much weight.

Obesity kills. It reduces the quality of your dog's life at the very least. Overweight Pomeranians have a greater likelihood of developing heart disease, diabetes, digestive disorders, high blood pressure, pancreatitis, or liver dysfunction. They can suffer from shortness of breath, decreased stamina and energy, and intolerance to heat. For such a tiny breed, excess weight is almost a guarantee of worsening patellar luxation in a dog already prone to this problem.

If your Pomeranian is overweight, love him enough to put him on a diet. The recipe for weight loss is pretty basic:

- Reduce caloric intake, increase caloric burn.
- Cut back on the quantity of food for each meal.
- Pour a little water on dry food, or add a salt-free, low-calorie rice cake to help your dog feel more full. Adding a small spoonful of plain, canned pumpkin can also increase the feeling of fullness with very few calories.
- Exercise your dog every day, or at least several times a week. Take him for longer walks or take him more often. If he has health problems that restrict his capacity for exercise, increase his daily activity a little at time, exercising for short periods but more often throughout the day. (If your Pom is overweight and has patellar luxation, ask your vet about an exercise plan that is safe for his orthopedic condition.)
- Offer low calorie treats like carrots, green beans, a slice of banana,

a bite of melon, berries, a little lick of fat-free yogurt, or buy bite-size, low-cal treats.

The commitment to keep your dog on a diet is harder than executing the plan itself. It's so difficult to resist those cute little pleading eyes, or the feeling that you're being unkind by not sharing a goody with your Pom. But for his welfare, feed him a healthy treat instead and keep him fit and trim.

TABLE MANNERS

As owner, it will be up to you to teach your dog appropriate meal time behavior since there is no Emily Pawst or Amy Pomeranianbilt.

You feed your dog on a regular basis so he doesn't have to beg for his supper. Likewise, don't allow him to beg for yours. Your dog has more of an opportunity to try and talk you into giving him the food off your plate if he has nothing better to do while you are eating. No matter what cute tricks he performs for a bite of your food, don't give him one. This reinforces begging behavior which can and usually will escalate to the point where he barks non-stop, paws at your legs, and may even steal your food.

One of the best ways to prevent—or stop—begging is to place your dog in his crate along with a fun toy while you have your dinner. You can also put up a baby gate that cuts off his access to the kitchen while you are cooking or dining. Another option is, once you have served yourself, to serve up his food, then place him in his crate to eat while you are eating too.

If you really can't resist the urge to share a bite of your dinner with your Pom, ask him to lie down in place and wait. Once you are finished eating you can reward him for being obedient with a little taste of a healthy food from your supper. Meal time can be used as an opportunity to practice basic commands such as "sit" and "stay." When your Pom responds to

Cute and fluffy, yes; roly-poly and overstuffed—no! Letting your Pom get too fat is not good for his health or appearance.

your commands correctly, offer him his own bowl while praising him enthusiastically.

In a multi-dog household, meal time etiquette should be compared to that of a formal dinner party: each dog must eat at his own appointed seat. Although housemates may normally get along well together, each dog needs his own bowl and separate eating space. Individual crates or feeding areas in the kitchen, or whichever room is the designated dog room, work well for this. Separating multiple dogs from one another during dinner will keep any one of them from having to share his dinner and thereby prevent any

Getting yourself and your Pom out for regular walks will improve both your physical and mental states.

growling, snapping or food hoarding, or a fight before it can get started. Also, it's the only way that you can make certain that any dog on a special diet gets exactly what he is supposed to eat.

Keep your dog's eating zone free from distractions like chores that will have you running in and out of the house, children at play, or loud, noisy appliances. He won't appreciate having his meal interrupted anymore than you would. Whether your dog eats with you or at his own set time, in his crate or the kitchen, place his food in his eating area and give him the time to eat.

Unless your Pom must have access to dry food at all times such as part of a plan for preventing hypoglycemia when he finishes his meal, take up his bowl and wash it. If he doesn't finish after sufficient time (15 to 20 minutes), pick up his bowl and put it away until the next meal (in the refrigerator if it contains food that can spoil, and discard if he doesn't eat it the next time you try to feed). Dawdling at dinner may sometimes develop into finicky eating habits.

Your dog doesn't have to empty his bowl every time he eats, but if his appetite decreases, this could be a sign that health problems are brewing. If your dog tends to be a little finicky or doesn't like eating that well, smell his food. Some picky eaters have keen senses of smell and if the odor of the food is not fresh, may refuse to eat. If this is the case, change his food for fresh or switch to a variety that has a better odor.

Although the cause may never be completely understood, there are other reasons why a dog may be picky eater. If health problems aren't the reason, and his food normally appeals to

The Telltale Signs of Obesity

Do you know if your Pomeranian is the right weight? Can't tell if he's just fluffy with fur or overweight? Here are some guidelines for checking.

Healthy Weight:
• Ribs can be felt through a minimal layer of fat padding, but are not visible;
• Waist is noticeable when seen from above, has a slight hourglass shape;
• Abdomen appears slightly "tucked up" when seen from the side.

Overweight:
• Ribs can still be felt but there is a noticeable layer of excess fat;
• Waist still slightly visible when seen from above but may approach width of ribs;
• Abdominal tuck still noticeable, but may approach level of ribs.

Obese:
• Ribs may be difficult or impossible to feel;
• Fat is thick, and visible around lower spine and base of the tail;
• Waist may be impossible to discern;
• Abdominal tuck is gone or may sag below level of ribs.

To ensure that your dog's weight is not going too far in the opposite direction, look for the opposite indications: Ribs, spine, and hips are prominently visible, when touched there is no padding; waist is exaggerated, and remaining muscle mass may be drawn into spaces between the ribs and spine; abdomen appears drawn in and tuck is also exaggerated.

If you're still not certain if your dog is overweight, ask your veterinarian. She can accurately tell you how much weight, if any, your Pom might need to lose.

Once your Poms have been weaned, they should each have their own food bowls so you can be sure every one of them is getting what they need.

him, your response should usually remain the same: give your dog the time to eat, and if he doesn't, remove his bowl. When he's hungry, he will eat. There are a few situations when missing a portion of a single meal could upset your dog's health, for example, if your Pom is one of those prone to low blood sugar. In such cases, your veterinarian may advise you about special techniques to use or foods to give to make certain your dog does not skip a necessary meal.

Just as with any other training, committing to a regular diet and meal plan, and consistently reinforcing proper meal time behavior is good for your dog's health and well-being. Your dog may never eat in a public restaurant, but when you have company for dinner, his table manners will make him a welcome guest, too.

5

GROOMING
Your Pomeranian

O ne of the most charming aspects of the Pomeranian is his beautiful, fluffy, full-bodied coat. It makes you want to wrap your hands around it and pet, stroke, cuddle the dog bearing this lustrous fur. Unfortunately the thick, double-coat of the Pom does not maintain itself. In order to retain this plush look, your Pom needs regular, thorough grooming sessions.

Commitment to owning a Pomeranian also means commitment to grooming. Although grooming a Pom is not as involved as grooming other breeds such as Poodles or Yorkshire Terriers, Pomeranians are nonetheless a moderately high-maintenance breed. Grooming a dog for the show ring requires even more experience, time, and effort. But for the pet owner, grooming is a task that can be learned and maintained at home.

Although you can learn to groom your own dog, whether or not he will be shown, it is still wise to plan for the time necessary to maintain his coat and to budget for grooming expenses, such as the purchase of brushes and shampoos. Even for those owners who opt to groom at home, an occasional trip to the groomer for a deep and thorough comb out, is a good idea; so remember to include this in your grooming budget, as well. The best way to keep your Pom looking his best is to be prepared to do the job and do it correctly throughout his life.

PREPARE FOR GROOMING BY HANDLING

The first step in maintaining that Pomeranian pouf is training. Dogs need to be trained to accept handling in order to be groomed, and the time to start is during puppyhood. Your puppy should permit you to handle him as needed. Prepare him by gently and regularly touching his feet, ears, tail, head, eye region, anal area, and his entire body. Handle and hold him in a manner similar to the types of touch you will use when he is groomed. Allow him to smell the surface where he will stand to be brushed, as well as the implements which you'll use on his coat. Reward him with praise, and maybe a small treat, when he accepts these touches and behaves well.

Some grooming, such as in the stomach area, is more easily

Get your Pom used to grooming when he's a puppy so that he learns it's a pleasant, rewarding experience.

accomplished if the dog lies on his side. Start training your Pom early to lie quietly while you handle him. As he gets used to the concentrated touching and the grooming tools, gradually increase the amount of time you work on him with each practice session. Add some strokes with a comb to the routine early on and offer praise when he behaves correctly.

"Dogs have different degrees of accepting grooming" explains Barbara Bird, a professional groomer from Arizona and founder of the informational website groomclassroom.com. "Pomeranians are lively and may jump around a lot. They 'dance,' move their feet, and can be hard to control, which makes it more difficult to groom them and more likely that the dog could be injured; so it's important to teach your dog to positively accept grooming."

Never punish your dog for not holding still, as this can teach him to dislike or be fearful of being groomed. Instead, offer praise or treats when he is calm and allows grooming; this teaches him to look forward to grooming sessions. If your Pom is one of those who, after training, is still a bit fussy or snappish about being groomed, Bird recommends trying a soft, firmly but comfortably fitted, nylon muzzle to calm him and prevent biting.

In some cases, such as adopted rescues who may not be used to regular grooming, the same methods can be used to help them adapt to the routine. An older dog who might never have received grooming attention may take longer to acclimate, particularly if he has been handled roughly in the past. With a positive, steady approach, some patience, and praise, most dogs learn to accept being groomed.

"Build the expectation of grooming into your dog's world. Don't wait until he has that big fluff of coat which requires more work. The time to start is before the coat needs any real effort to groom it," says Bird. "Grooming time needs to be separate from play and snuggle time. It's another form of attention, but not to be confused with fun. This doesn't mean it has to be awful, the dog just needs to learn to accept it as part of his life."

GROOMING SUPPLIES

In order to more efficiently get the job done, it is important to have the correct equipment for grooming your Pomeranian. Purchase the best tools that you can afford. Brushes and combs that are cheap wear out quickly, and the surfaces of poorly-made bristles or teeth can damage fur. Select stainless steel or non-stick surface combs with medium- to wider-spaced teeth. Smaller toothed combs may not be best for Pom fur, except for finishing work in the facial or feet areas.

Combs with rotating teeth are available for aiding in mat removal. Some owners like this type, while others feel that the rotation can cause tangling. Slickers are useful for removing debris from the coat and for fluffing. A pin brush, with polished tips, is the preferred tool for grooming a Pomeranian, so choose one that is well made.

Don't forget to include a doggy toothbrush and toothpaste in your grooming kit. Choose an appropriate trimmer for nails, as well. Along with trimmers, purchase some styptic powder. With the need to keep fur trimmed away from the feet and anal area, another helpful grooming tool is a small, electric or rechargeable hair clipper, designed for trimming hair around the pads of the feet.

A grooming table with an arm and break-away noose makes the job of maintaining your Pomeranian much easier. Over-the-table support systems are available which secure the rear of the dog as well, and help to minimize "dancing," which is especially important

Grooming as a Health Check

Grooming time is the perfect opportunity to give your dog a quick check up for signs that something may be going amiss with his health.

- During brushing, does the fur feel and look healthy? Does your dog seem overly sensitive to discomfort?

- In the bath, run your hands over every inch of his body. Are there any lumps or bumps that should not be there? Is the fur or skin too dry or too oily?

- Are the ears clean? Is there an unusual quantity of wax? Does either ear smell badly? Do the eyes have an excessive quantity of tears or is there a mucousy or discolored discharge?

- Blow-dryers part fur down to the bare skin. Look closely while drying your dog. Are there any discolorations? Is the skin scaly or flaky?

- Nail trimming is a good time to check between the pads for briars or burrs that need removal. Check for cuts or abrasions on the pads that may require first aid.

- Observe your healthy dog while grooming him. This establishes a baseline against which you can judge in the future what is normal and what is unhealthy.

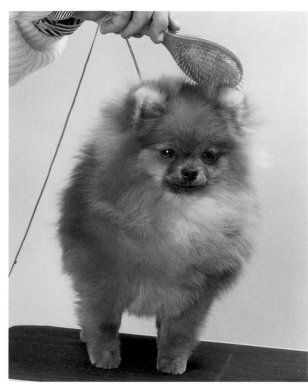

This Pom is being groomed on a table, which makes it easier for his owner to get to all parts of his body equally.

while you are using scissors. Tables provide a consistent space to which your dog
can become accustomed when you work on him.

For after the bath, owners should also consider purchasing a high-velocity dryer that "knocks" the water out of the coat and straightens fur as it dries without the use of excess heat which can dry the coat and skin. Those who wish to do complete, detailed grooming need a pair or two of high-quality scissors of different varieties, such as blending shears, for trimming and shaping. A set of professional clippers with the proper blades in their grooming kit may prove useful as well.

The choice of shampoo should be one that deep cleans the thick coat without drying the fur or skin but does not cause the fur to lose body and become limp. Pet shampoos come in a wider range of pH than do shampoos for people. Also, additives in human shampoos, like fragrances, coloring, and other enhancing ingredients, could cause irritation, damage the coat, or cause loss of body. For some Poms, a conditioner may keep their skin from becoming too dry. But avoid products with heavy moisturizers which may excessively soften the stand-off, stand-up coat, causing it to lay flat instead.

"You don't want to take out the crispness," says Bird, "I recommend using a product that contains dimethicone or cyclomethicone. These ingredients have the capacity to cling to and smooth the rough edges of the fur's cuticle without removing body, and they add the appearance of reflected light which will enhance the fur without drying the skin." Before using a silicone-based product on your Pom, discuss your grooming methods with your breeder. Some breeders who do extensive grooming on their show Poms believe that silicone ingredients, such as cyclomethicone, cause too much heat to be conducted into the fur during drying. However, if your dryer uses cool air this should not be an issue.

BRUSHING & COMBING

Brushing is necessary to remove dead hair that becomes trapped in the fur. During periods of shedding, extra brushing will be necessary to prevent the hair that is being lost from causing mats. Poms have soft undercoats which can get matted, especially under the ruff and around the "pantaloons." The goal in brushing is to get into the coat deeply enough to remove debris and loose fur and to prevent the coat from pelting or clumping.

To begin grooming your Pomeranian, place him on the grooming table. If you have not purchased a table especially for grooming, you can improvise by placing a non-skid rug on top of a counter, folding table or even the washer or dryer.

Lightly mist the coat before brushing or combing to prevent damage. A mixture of one ounce of conditioner to one cup water, stored in a spray bottle is a good method for pre-brush misting. Don't saturate the fur, only dampen it. If you prefer not to work with damp fur, try using corn starch instead.

Before you begin brushing, you may wish to place a little baby powder behind the ears and around the anal area to absorb natural body oils that can spread through the fur, attract dirt, and possibly cause the coat to mat.

Methods and brushing sequences vary by groomer or owner, but some generally-accepted guidelines are suggested. Line-brushing—vertically separating a line of fur, working it out, then moving to the next line—is one good way to give your Pom a thorough brushing, often starting at the shoulder and working back, or from the belly and working up. Whichever method you use, always work with small sections at a time. Brush first, then comb.

Bird likes to brush from the outside in and comb from the inside, next to the skin, out. "You don't want to leave coat that hasn't been combed, next to the skin," she explains, "This is the most common problem in home grooming, and it can cause the undercoat to clump. That's why brushing by itself isn't sufficient unless you are really experienced."

If you do encounter a mat, hold the fur next to the skin to keep it from pulling. Gently try to separate the mat with your fingers.

Before beginning to brush your Pom, spray his coat lightly with a water/conditioner mix.

Then, starting at the bottom of the mat, comb through to the end of the fur. Next, move higher up into the mat and carefully work the comb down again to the end. This method prevents the tangle from tightening. Repeat until the mat is removed.

Before or After?

For years, grooming wisdom taught that in order to prevent mats, dogs must be brushed before bathing. This was practical advice because mats can tighten if they become wet. But according to Bird, this is now considered the "old school" way of grooming.

"As a professional groomer, I mostly prefer to work on a clean, conditioned coat—in other words —a protected coat. Today's products are less likely to cause mats to worsen if you don't brush them out before bathing. If you tackle a matted coat when it's dry and dirty, it may cause the hair to break or it may pull out more coat," Bird says. "If there are large areas of mats, for example if the dog's entire rear end is a mass of mats, then you might want to do some pre-bath work, using a spray-in conditioner, and dividing the mats to create smaller hunks that can then be finished after bathing."

BATHING & DRYING

Get out the doggy shampoo, conditioner, towels, table, dryer, and tools and have them all ready before placing your dog in the water. Chasing a wet, shaking dog around the house is frustrating and makes for a messy grooming session.

Pomeranians are small enough that it may be more convenient to bathe them in a kitchen or laundry sink rather than in a traditional tub. A walk-in shower stall which has a built-in seat may also be easier for bathing your dog. Attach a sprayer hose to your faucet if you do not already have one plumbed in for regular use. Adjust the water to a comfortably warm temperature, not so cool it might chill your dog and not so hot that it burns. A cotton ball placed in each ear may prevent water from entering, and a light coating of petroleum jelly smeared over the delicate membranes of the eyes can help keep soap out.

With your dog facing away from the sprayer, and with the stream of water directed away from his face, lift his head in your hand and gently begin wetting him from the top of his head, moving towards his tail. Work backwards and down, always keeping the stream of water pointed towards the bottom of the sink so that it is less likely to run into your dog's ears and eyes. Continue wetting the underside of your dog by spraying at a downwards angle across his chest and stomach, and between his front and back legs. The coat is adequately saturated when a little more water than a drip runs from the fur in all areas.

Prior to pouring it on the fur, shampoo should be mixed with enough water so that it runs easily throughout the coat without having to be worked in, which can cause the fur to clump. Apply sufficient shampoo that it lathers easily, but not so much that it is difficult to rinse out. Start on the back, then the sides. Tip the head up and backward to apply a small amount of shampoo to the top of the head and the neck area. Place some shampoo in your palm to help direct it more easily onto the chest, belly, and between the back legs. Be careful around the eyes, ears, and genitals. Lather the shampoo with single-motion strokes, moving in the same direction as the fur to reduce the chance of creating tangles. Rinse thoroughly. If you are using a conditioner, apply in the same manner as the shampoo and according to the directions. Again, rinse thoroughly.

If you teach your dog to "shake off" the excess water first, drying him will be easier. Shaking off water is a natural instinct, so when your dog does shake, just praise and reward him while using the phrase "shake off" to enforce the behavior. Next, place a medium-thick towel over the body, except for the face, and gently squeeze the moisture from the coat without rubbing, once again moving from the head backwards and down. Carefully but thoroughly dry the ears to prevent water from draining into the ear canal and possibly causing an infection.

It is preferable that the Pomeranian's thick coat not be allowed to air dry. If the weather is humid, the undercoat may not dry and hot spots could form. Using a dog dryer or handheld blow dryer set on no- or low heat, blow the coat dry, blowing against the direction of the coat, from back to front. Brush while drying, brushing from the tail towards the head and from the stomach up towards the back. This fluffs the coat and helps it to stand up, creating that stand-off look for which the Pomeranian is known. Bathing, drying, and brushing your dog will take about 60 to 90 minutes, longer if you are preparing him for the show ring.

Have a supply of thick towels handy for when you finish washing your Pom. They can soak up a lot of the water before you have to brush and dry him.

FREQUENCY OF GROOMING

How often you brush and bathe your Pomeranian depends on his health, activity level, and environment. In between baths or visits to a groomer, your Pomeranian needs to be brushed and maybe combed. Recommendations vary on how often this is necessary, ranging from daily, to several times a week, to weekly, or whenever needed. Brushing or combing may only take 15 minutes if your Pom's coat is kept in good condition.

Frequency of bathing differs. Show dogs tend to be bathed more often, as do dogs who play outside a great deal. Couch potatoes without skin problems won't need bathing as frequently. Owners may find that baths could be needed once a week (be careful not to make the skin and fur too dry!), once a month, or even three or four times a year. If your dog's coat feels grimy to the touch, if he has an odor, or if there is dirt in the coat, then it's time for a bath. Judge what works best for your dog and plan time for these grooming sessions in your schedule.

Grooming as Bonding

Before they even open their eyes, puppies are used to being groomed by their mothers. Their mother's tongue cleans them throughout the day and night—and makes them feel secure. Even in wild canids, mutual grooming is used from puppyhood into adulthood as a ritual that unites the pack.

Some dogs like routine. This includes their grooming, as well. The routine becomes predictable and recognizable. By following an order and schedule, the periodic distress that might be associated with grooming becomes more acceptable. If you offer a few treats as a reward for being good during grooming, your dog can learn to enjoy it. Plus, he will love the time that you are spending with him.

When you groom your dog, he instinctively remembers the nurturing sensation from when he was a baby. Just like dog-to-dog bonding, the time spent grooming your Pomeranian binds you to each other in a relationship of mutual respect, better health, and love.

HAIR TRIMMING

As a Nordic type dog, Pomeranians are considered a "natural" breed, meaning that their visual appearance is more as they naturally have looked for centuries and less modified by humans as part of their breeding. As such, according to grooming tradition, they are supposed to be shown in a more natural state, without excessive trimming. Trimming, as a grooming technique, can be anything from the removal of a very few, scraggly hairs to total shaping or styling, such as with the Bichon or Poodle.

Today, trimming—where, how much, and to what extent—is one of the greatest controversies in Pomeranian conformation show rings around the world.

In general, it is acceptable, common practice to trim away the hair around the feet and on up the legs a little ways. It is also alright to cut excess or long hair from the ear, and to remove stray or scraggly hairs that stick up and look out of place. Because they do have such thick, long hair, it is not only accepted, but highly recommended to keep the fur trimmed away from the anal area for the sake of cleanliness.

From there, trimming practices and recommendations are all over the board. In some countries, including Canada, trimming is highly objectionable. European standards change frequently, and during certain times the Pom standard may have an expressed caveat against trimming.

US handlers are often criticized because of the stylized manner in which coated dogs are groomed and shown. Pomeranians in the show ring in the States are beautifully sculpted by trimming to enhance the dog's natural shape, play down faults in build, and to emphasize strong points.

For most owners, learning how to trim a show dog, and deciding how much and where to trim will not be an issue. If you do plan to show your Pom, learn from the best. Visit a groomer who is experienced in trimming the show Pomeranian, have your breeder show you how, and go to a dog show and observe how the professional handlers do it.

Owners of pet Pomeranians just need to be concerned with keeping debris out of their dogs' coats, keeping them from matting, and reducing the chance of slippage when they walk. Trimming generally permissible for all show Poms is: feet, lower pasterns and hocks (the lower portions of the front and back legs), between the pads of the feet, or anywhere the coat may drag and pick up debris or rub and tangle.

Clipping

Some owners may prefer to clip their Pom into a shorter cut. There are several reasons why: if a dog's coat is open, long and scraggly, and tends to mat easily; if there is a perception that the dog is too hot or needs a cut for health reasons; if a different look is desired; or grooming often enough is not possible and an easier-to-maintain cut is needed. Shorter styles can include a lion clip, a teddy bear cut, or just a shorter look.

Caution is advised when clipping back that Pom coat. First, fur not only serves as an insulator against cold, it also protects against excess heat. Dogs whose fur has been clipped too short can be more susceptible to becoming chilled or over-heated far more quickly and easily than a full-coated dog, even in summer.

Also, with the Pomeranian coat, once it is clipped short, it may grow back in with a fuzzier or more wiry texture, eventually rendering the coat incapable of growing back correctly. Additionally, with a disposition to fur loss, Poms may suffer "clip alopecia," a condition of unknown cause that may damage hair follicles and prevent them from regrowing new hair

This show dog has been masterfully groomed so that every hair is in place.

following a close cut or shave. So before you decide to clip your Pom's fur short, discuss it with your breeder and groomer.

EAR CARE

With their perky, upright ears, Pomeranians do not commonly suffer with ear infections as easily as do the drop-eared breeds like Basset Hounds or Cocker Spaniels, but this does not mean that ear care can be forgotten. When you are grooming your Pom, remember to check his ears. They should be clean and free from wax and debris, and the skin lining the ear should be a healthy color, not red or irritated looking. If you do find wax in the ear, gently wipe it away using the tip of your finger covered with a soft cloth. Always be careful when you are working within the ear, not to go too deeply as this may cause damage and pain.

Some Poms may have extra or excessively thick hair growing around their ears. This can be removed, but do so with caution. Use blunt-tipped, curved scissors to cut away the excess while placing your finger over the skin of the ear to prevent accidental cuts.

EYE CARE

Eyes should be clear and bright, and free from discharge. With either the eyes or ears, if redness, discharge, or excessive build-up is present, it's time for a veterinary exam.

Tear Stains

In some light-colored Pomeranians, there may be a slight tendency for the dog to experience tear staining. These stains appear as pinkish, ruddy, or brownish streaks around the eye where tears naturally drain. Causes are varied, including allergies, ingredients in drinking water, or possibly an irritation of the eye caused by dryness or even eyelashes. Discolored tears can actually stain fur.

Washing the eye area with a cotton ball moistened with warm water or sterile saline (like humans that wear contacts use) helps

Finding a Groomer

Finding a qualified and caring professional to groom your Pomeranian should be undertaken with many of the same considerations you would apply in selecting a kennel or veterinarian. Important considerations include:

- Is the groomer certified by a reputable board?
- Do they have sufficient experience in thier trade to groom a Pomeranian?
- Are they experienced with dogs and do they understand their behavior?
- Are their prices reasonable? Competitive?
- Is the grooming facility clean? Are the grooming implements cleaned between each use?
- Does the groomer competently and happily handle special requests?
- Do other dogs present appear relaxed or anxious?
- Is the groomer considerate of and patient with the dogs on whom they work?
- Do they like dogs and enjoy the work?
- Are they willing to give you a tour, or meet your dog and talk with you before you make an appointment?

reduce staining and may be done whenever needed. Products specifically for removal of tear stains are available from pet supply stores. Use these products according to the directions.

Make sure to have your dog's eyes examined by your veterinarian to determine the cause of his tearing, and get treatment if necessary.

NAIL CARE

Part of routine grooming for all dogs is trimming toenails. This usually needs to be done about every two weeks. Several types of nail clippers are available for dogs, but many groomers recommend the plier-type versus the guillotine type because they are less likely to cause discomfort from pinching the nail. Choosing the most appropriate size trimmer is also important. A few Poms may be small enough to have their nails trimmed with cat nail clippers, but these trimmers are made for very tiny nails and may possibly pinch even the Pom's small nails. Whichever size or type you choose, a set with a nail guard may be helpful in preventing cutting into the quick. Nail grinders are another easy way to keep doggy toenails trimmed, but could cause problems such as pulled fur, or tenderness if small Pom nails are ground too quickly.

Tearing and staining around the eyes can be a problem for lighter-colored Poms. Washing can reduce the staining, but a persistent problem should be referred to your veterinarian.

Before trimming your dog's nails, use a small set of fur clippers or a pair of curved-blade, blunt-tipped scissors to cut away excess hair around the pads and bottom of the feet. After the feet are done, steady the dog with your body and gently but firmly grasp a paw with one hand while operating the clippers with the other. Hold the blades at about a 45-degree angle away from the bottom of the foot and snip the toenail at the point where it curves, being careful not to pinch or cut into the quick, the tender and sensitive, blood-rich bed around which the nail grows.

If your dog has clearish-white nails, you will be able to easily see the pink of the quick and avoid cutting into it. But most Poms have dark nails, so carefully nip a little bit of nail at a time working slowly back, stopping just before a heavier, white layer of nail shows through the bottom center of the nail.

Should you nick the quick accidentally, it will bleed and your dog may yelp or snap. Without making a big fuss, apologize, reassure him that he is fine, and move on. Stop the bleeding with styptic powder or by placing the foot in a container of corn starch. If you are worried that you can't trim your dog's nails without hurting him, ask your groomer or a veterinary technician to demonstrate for you how to trim the toenails.

DENTAL CARE

Just like people, dogs need to have their teeth brushed after eating. It may not be practical to brush them after every meal, but it is important to clean them as frequently as possible. Pomeranians are quite prone to dental problems, including tooth decay and loss, so plan to brush your dog's teeth a minimum of once weekly. If at all possible, daily brushing is preferred. Providing safe chew toys that aid in plaque removal and prevent tartar buildup is another way to help keep your Pom's teeth clean.

A large selection of doggy toothbrushes, fingertip brushes, and powdered or paste cleaners are available. Never use human toothpaste, since it is not safe to swallow, and dogs will swallow whatever you use to clean their teeth. Choose whichever products keep your Pom's teeth the cleanest, are easy to use, and which your dog most readily tolerates. For the Pomeranian's tiny mouth, a child-size toothbrush may be a good fit.

One method to help your dog cooperate during teeth cleaning is to start by wrapping your finger with a piece of gauze dipped in doggy toothpaste. Later, when he is used to having your finger in his mouth, move on to a toothbrush. Brush your dog's teeth during a regular grooming session while he is still on the table. In between groomings, if he is calm, you can hold him in your lap with one hand and use your other hand to clean his teeth.

Safely trimming a Pom's nails requires snipping away any excess fur around the toes and using the proper-sized clipping instrument or a nail grinder.

Because of the breed's dental problems (see Chapter 8) it is vital to your Pom's health not to overlook brushing the teeth as part of his regular routine. Always remember to keep your dog's teeth healthy and white.

· POUF YOUR POM

Keeping the Pomeranian looking like a Pomeranian is an effort that requires time, money, and commitment. Show or pet, full-coated or clipped like a teddy bear, the Pomeranian is not a dog whose grooming can be ignored. This is a breed that needs work, but the effort is worth it to those who care for and truly love the Pom.

In addition to the poufy picture of beauty your dog presents after being groomed, the hours you spend grooming deepen the bond between you and your dog. Bird summarizes, "Grooming is a meditation that requires a great deal of patience, and a way for the dogs to get loving attention from their owners." Show your Pom you love him—groom him when he needs it. Just remember these dogs are sensitive, so groom with a careful hand.

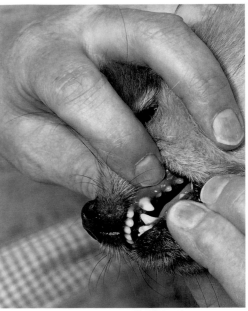

Keeping your Pom's teeth and jaws healthy should be a top concern. Work around his mouth gently and with toothpaste that he'll like, and he will learn the procedure is painless—and tasty.

Doggie Bad Breath

Your dog loves you and jumps into your lap to show you how much. He licks your face and breathes on you and—yuck—doggy breath! Not much smells worse than bad breath from a dog. But Pomeranian breath doesn't have to reek. Some tips for making your Pom's breath as pleasant as his personality are:

- Keep his teeth clean. Brush frequently and have veterinary dental cleanings when your dog gets tartar build-up.

  - Don't feed food that has an unpleasant odor. Premium food with high-grade ingredients is less likely to cause death-breath. And dry food causes less breath odor than canned.

  - Toys and treats that offer teeth-cleaning action and breath-freshening properties are readily available from pet supply stores.

  - Get a veterinary exam. Many diseases, dental problems, and other health conditions can cause bad breath. Top among these are kidney, liver or lung disease, and canine malignant melanoma, an aggressive cancer that forms mainly in the mouth.

TRAINING AND BEHAVIOR
of Your Pomeranian

How do wild, rowdy puppies grow into good, well-mannered dogs? By training that starts early—before you even get a dog! Prior to bringing home an adorable Pom, owners first need to research and understand the traits and temperament of the breed, and study dog behavior so that those bewildering puppy mannerisms are more easily understood. If you understand general dog behavior, it is less likely that your puppy will become a problem dog in the future. Training your dog will also be easier if you understand how Poms tend to behave.

TRAINING IS IMPORTANT

Being able to turn a Pomeranian into a well-behaved member of your family or a model of canine good citizenship begins the moment you walk through the door and establish the tone for acceptable behavior. The earlier you begin, the easier it is to shape your dog's manners. Teaching a puppy how to live with you in your home goes far beyond feeding and housetraining. It requires a daily endeavor that establishes the ground rules for your Pom and forms the basis for a lifetime of good behavior.

Dogs are quick studies and can learn a new behavior almost every day—even if it's only learning how not to get caught when they break a housetraining rule. It's easier to train as you go than to untrain a dog's bad habits. You teach your dog bad habits if you ignore a problem when it arises. Don't encourage behavior in a pup that you will not tolerate for his entire life. Don't confuse your dog by accepting a behavior one day, then changing the rules tomorrow. In other words, don't

The earlier you begin teaching your puppy right from wrong in a positive, rewarding way, the sooner you'll have a well-behaved Pomeranian.

permit your Pom to engage in behavior which he will later have to unlearn, then relearn the correct behavior.

Since dogs don't come pre-trained and knowing exactly what is expected of them in your home, it's up to you to teach them in a loving manner which behaviors are correct and which are not. In the first days after his homecoming, while the relationship between you and your Pom is just being forged, you may be surprised—but delighted—to discover that one of the most important reasons to train your dog is because the interaction that comes through training will bond you and your dog closely to each other.

TRAINING FOR MANNERS & MORE

We live with dogs because they're beautiful to behold, fun to play with, and mostly because we love them and they love us. They're a joy to be around...if they are good dogs. Dogs that behave badly are not so much a pleasure as they are a pain. Even the extra-adorable Pom needs to be well-mannered in order to be a joy with which to live.

To your dog, your home is his den and your family is his pack. Just like in a pack, there are rules for acceptable behavior which he must learn. He must also learn to fit into his place in the family structure, with you as the head of the pack. This is pack hierarchy, a "pecking order" which dogs understand and respect.

Good doggy manners can compare to well-behaved children who act appropriately in any home or public place. Of course this means housetraining, but it also means abiding by house rules, being polite with company, good table manners, and getting along with others—of multiple species.

Specifically, you will need to determine what the rules are going to be for your dog in your home. Will he be allowed on the furniture? When guests arrive, do you want to him lie down calmly until you give a signal that he may greet them? Is he supposed to stay out of the trash? Should he to remain quiet when he rides in the car? Some owners may not mind if their dogs bark their heads off when on an outing, or if they jump up on them when they return home, but if this is unacceptable behavior for your Pomeranian, either in private or in public, then you will need to teach him how to act.

Even though Poms like to be in charge, your dog will look to you first for clues on how to behave, and for you to be the leader. Don't disappoint him. Set the rules and abide by them. Just make certain they are reasonable and fair. Be consistent in when and where you enforce the rules. Don't let a cute look and wagging tail con you into accepting bad behavior.

Remember, if you don't take the lead and give your Pom guidance, he will assume command and make up his own rules as he goes along. If he decides to grab a morsel from your breakfast plate and you laugh at how precious he looks eating your buttered toast in the middle of your sofa, you have conveyed to him that it's acceptable to do this. In his mind he will see this as meaning that he's now in charge and can do as he pleases, and have what he wants, when and where he wants. You've reinforced bad manners and placed his pack status above your own.

As incredible as dogs are, they are not capable of running a household. Your Pomeranian's confidence and security, and his ability to be a well-behaved companion, all hinge upon your ability to be a strong leader and good teacher. Dogs who believe that they are in charge, and are allowed to behave as they please are not just problem dogs—they are under stress and stressed dogs are not happy dogs. Heading up your pack is a lot of pressure to put on such a small creature.

As confident and independent as a Pomeranian can be, it is not his job to run your household. In fact, he will be happier if you establish yourself as his "leader."

Despite a streak of willfulness and a penchant to persist in obtaining his own way, the Pom usually prefers to receive his owner's hearty approval. By telling him precisely what you expect, showing him how to do (or not do) what you want and then lavishing him with praise when he obeys, your dog will blossom into a well-mannered companion.

It's also important to remember that since your dog is part of the family, it is essential that every member of your household understand and abide by the "pack" rules. Although one individual should be primarily responsible for determining these rules, everyone else needs to agree with them and support your dog's learning process.

CRATE TRAINING

Before your new Pom comes through your door for the first time, you should have his own space ready and waiting for him. A crate is a "room" for your dog, just like a bedroom is for a child. Crates are not little prisons for dogs. They are a safe and secure, personal haven where your dog can eat, retreat, rest, recover, and even play in peace. Selecting the proper crate should be near the top of your list of things to do before bringing your new dog home.

Position your Pom's crate in a location that is dry, warm, and free from drafts in the winter, but equally pleasant in the summer months. Your dog should be able to see, or at least hear and smell you from his crate. It should be in a room where you spend much of your time, such as your bedroom. With a young puppy, it is best to set up the crate near your bed at night. Other possible locations are the kitchen or a family room, places that are central to household activities, conveniently close to feeding and a door to the dog yard, but not in the way of traffic from people entering or leaving the house.

Once you have placed the crate and prepared it (see Chapter 3), you will need to teach your dog that this is his own, special place. Show him that it is a space he can enjoy just for himself. Entice him into the crate for the first time by putting a few treats in the back. Allow him to wander in on his own, sniff the space and wander back out. Don't shove him in and shut the door. A couple of safe toys will make the crate a place where he wants to stay. Feeding him his meals in the crate will also help your Pom realize that his crate is a good place to be.

How long it takes your dog to accept the crate as his personal space varies. Some dogs become attached to their crates immediately,

Hitting Is Not Training

Owners frustrated with a dog who repeatedly does something they do not want him to do may resort to slapping their dog in an attempt to teach him to stop the behavior. Although a rolled newspaper and a whack on the side, head, or rump used to be considered an acceptable "training method," it is not. Hitting a dog is never appropriate.

An inexperienced, first-time owner, or someone from the "old-school" of dog training may question why, particularly if a smack has achieved a temporary reprieve from the undesirable behavior. The reason is because hitting is not training, it's punishment.

You have not taught your dog correct or acceptable behavior if you hit him. You have taught him to fear you, and to fear your hands or whatever item, like a newspaper, you use to swat him.

The appropriate response to frustrating or unacceptable behavior is to show your dog what the correct behavior is instead. Analyze why your dog is doing what he is doing. Once you understand the reason—from his point of view—you can figure out a way to redirect his actions into behavior that is acceptable to both of you, and which makes sense to your dog.

Dogs do not understand being hit; there is no equivalent in canine behavior. Instead of an angry, physical response, when your dog engages in the behavior you don't want, stop him with an "eh, eh" sound, then show him what you do want him to do. Praise him immediately when he responds correctly. Each time he repeats the undesired action, redirect the behavior, then praise. Keep doing this until he gets the idea.

Because dogs may engage in activities which seem perfectly reasonable to them, but may go against your personal preferences, it is up to you to provide your dog with a way to understand the diversion of his natural desires. Teach him how to live in your home following your rules and acting as you prefer, but do it without hitting; do it with respect, patience, and persistence.

particularly if their breeder used crates with her dogs. Others may take a few days to get used to the concept, and a few may resist, pawing at the door and barking to get out every time you latch the door.

This isn't because your dog is claustrophobic. Claustrophobia can occur in dogs, but it is extremely rare. Most dogs just want to get out to be with you, to explore or play somewhere else, or to engage in another activity. Because crate-training is a cornerstone to good behavior, including housetraining, it's important that you continue to work with your Pom in order to teach him to accept his crate. Don't give in to your dog's efforts to convince you that being in his crate is a terrible torture which he cannot survive. Gently tap your finger against the front-top of the crate and tell him, "settle" or "quiet." When he calms down, even if it's only for a short while, you can praise him and let him out. Continue working with him to accept his crate by placing him back into it again with a few treats.

If you set up your Pom's crate to be a comfortable and safe place, he will soon want to escape to it on his own. It will be his private refuge.

As your dog adapts to the routine and enters his crate on his own, praise him. When you first begin crate training use a phrase like, "get in your crate" or "go to bed," while gently directing him into the crate where a few treats await him. Soon he will begin to associate your request with being crated, as well enjoy being there. Gradually increase the amount of time your dog rests in his crate, until he is used to being crated quietly for at least an hour or two.

Crates are not a substitute for supervising your dog or taking care of him. Puppies need a potty break about every two hours; adult dogs should not be crated more than fours hours at a time without a break. Even with outdoor breaks, your dog should not be crated longer than a total of eight to nine hours a day, except for during the night beside your bed, when he is very young. Even then, it is likely he will need a mid-night trip outdoors to relieve himself.

Besides serving as your dog's den, a crate will help keep him safe and out of trouble when you can't watch him, A crate also provides him a space where he can get away from activity when the household is busy, and keep him from escaping or getting stepped on when company visits. The crate is not only your Pom's home in miniature, it is an excellent training tool which should soon become one of your dog's favorite places.

HOUSETRAINING

Puppies are little urine and feces factories. Put even a little food or water in the front end and in a short while far less pleasant substances are guaranteed to come out the back—preferably not inside on your floors. There's nothing quite as inconvenient, embarrassing, and destructive about a puppy as finding one of their piddle puddles soaked into the carpet.

Reliable housetraining is one of the most important lessons an owner can teach a dog. Although it is probably the most time-consuming and tedious training job that you tackle, it is critical that you don't take any shortcuts, overlook mishaps, or accept failure in the early stages. To do so practically ensures a lifetime of wet, smelly stains on your carpet.

Puppies confined to a space where they do not want to eliminate and who are regularly taken to a place where they are rewarded for doing their business, soon learn what is expected of them.

Housetraining a Puppy

Before you bring your puppy home, designate an outdoor area for him to use as his "toilet." Access from indoors should be convenient to reaching the spot in all types weather. If you use a different door other than the one he exits for play, walks or rides, it may help your dog understand that this means it's time for him to do his business. Ideally, your dog's potty area will also be located close to where you can efficiently dispose of feces when you clean the yard.

Right from the first moment you bring your new dog home, take him directly to his spot and allow him to investigate and smell it thoroughly. Give him a sufficient chance to relieve himself on his own, but don't stay so long he becomes confused as to why he's there. Encourage him to "go potty." If he does, praise him exuberantly as if he has achieved something amazing and wonderful—which he has. Just don't be so enthusiastic that you scare him. If your dog doesn't potty after awhile, take him inside and crate him.

Crates serve as excellent housetraining tools by teaching your puppy bladder and bowel control. Dogs are born with a natural instinct to keep their dens clean. When your puppy is confined in his crate he will avoid eliminating in order not to soil himself or his sleeping area. However, keep in mind that a puppy has limited control and storage capacity and needs to be taken out frequently, which means a young Pom will usually need to urinate at least every two hours, and after he eats, after he has a treat, after playing, after napping, in the morning when he wakes up, and at night before he goes to bed.

Whenever you let your puppy out of his crate, take him straight to his toilet area. You can't just put him outside and hope he goes; you have to go with him to make certain that he does. It is absolutely essential that you praise, praise, praise him when he does potty. Praise him so much that you sound silly and your neighbors think you are crazy. Your puppy must clearly realize that his relieving himself outdoors makes him a good dog and you an ecstatic owner. A little treat offered as reward may help reinforce the behavior with some Pomeranians.

Pomeranians and the 5 Ps

Prevent, provide, prohibit, practice, and praise. This simple-to-follow formula was devised and is recommended by Barbara McClatchey, a Texas obedience instructor with multiple Pomeranians.

Prevent. The first and maybe most important step is to prevent the dog from having the opportunity to do the unwanted behavior. Says McClatchey, "This means if you don't want your dog to chew your dirty laundry, don't leave it where he can get to it—keep him from gaining access to the forbidden items."

Provide. This means substituting an acceptable activity which is of equal interest to him as the undesired behavior. In other words, if he's chewing on a shoe, give him a toy that piques his interest even more.

Prohibit. Stop your dog from engaging in the incorrect behavior as soon as you see him doing it – or even thinking about doing it. (Remember, no hitting or yelling, or punishing after the fact.) Stopping undesirable behavior in the act is the prohibit step.

Practice. McClatchey also suggests that the dog should next be given an opportunity to do something correctly. Practice a command that he knows and does well. Follow through on the command; don't let your dog get away with not responding correctly.

Praise. Finally, and just as important as the first step, is praise. When he does as you request, or engages in a behavior that is correct, always tell your dog, in an enthusiastic manner, that he has done well.

Don't play with your puppy or allow him to wander around exploring while you are waiting for him to empty his bladder. He needs to understand the difference between play time and potty time. If he doesn't go when you take him out and give him the command, "go potty," return him to his crate and try again in 30 minutes or so. Your puppy must earn the privilege of staying out of his crate by eliminating outside.

Once he has pottied, he can remain outside his crate for exercise, play, and snuggling. But you must not let him out of your sight, as he needs to be observed every single second for any indication that he's about to empty his bladder. Puppies often realize quite suddenly that they need to urinate without giving you much warning. But if you are watching, you should notice at least some subtle signs such as a rapid shift in attention, sniffing, circling, running back and forth, a sudden burst of frantic activity, or an awkward movement that looks as if he's trying to decide if he wants to sit down. Rush him to his toilet spot and instruct him to "go potty" if you see any of these or other signals.

Fortunately, the signs that your puppy is about to evacuate his bowels occur on a more regular basis, usually within a few minutes to an hour after eating, and are more easily detected. Dogs about to defecate usually walk in a pattern, such as a circle, and hunch their back up while bending into a partial squat. When you see your puppy start to do this, get him outside quickly. Or better yet, take him out after he finishes eating.

Even though it may be time for your dog to go back into his crate, if he has just pottied, allow him a few more minutes of freedom so he learns that pottying outdoors means he gets more time out of his crate with you and his toys.

Confinement

Confinement is a key element in teaching your Pom where it is acceptable for him to eliminate and where it is not. Start with his crate, then a room, and eventually the rest of the house. As your puppy gets the idea that your entire home is also his den and must be kept free of his waste, you can gradually expand the areas where he is allowed as long as he remains under your watchful supervision. Do not permit him into more space than you can watch until he is reliably potty trained.

One way to insure constant supervision is the "umbilical" method. Put a puppy harness on your Pom and clip it to a long lead which is tethered to your belt, belt loop, waist, or wrist. Your dog will be where you can always see him yet able to play as he likes while you are likewise able to engage in other activities. When he moves, you can tell if he is just playing or about to relieve himself,

Teaching Old Dogs New Housetraining Habits

What happens to a puppy if he is confined to a kennel or exercise pen and ignored when he needs to relieve himself? What about a rescued dog who may have spent most of his former life in a small cage or banished to a basement? Under such circumstances, any normally clean dog can lose the natural instinct to keep his "den" clean.

Despite extreme effort to keep from soiling, eventually any dog will have to eliminate in his space if he is confined too long. And out of necessity, eventually he will accept this soiling as natural.

A Pomeranian from these situations can be retrained, but it will present a greater challenge, requiring more time and effort than it would usually take to housetrain a puppy from stage one. First, make the dog's personal space in his crate as small as possible while still maintaining comfort. The dog will need to be taken out more often and at the least little sign that he might even be thinking about relieving himself. When he does potty outdoors, give effusive praise along with multiple bites of his favorite treat. This helps impress upon him the positive outcome for changing his habits.

When he eliminates in his crate, do not show anger or displeasure with your dog. Promptly remove him, take him outdoors, and proceed with routine housetraining steps. Placing an item scented with the urine or feces from his mishap in the desired elimination spot may help teach him where his approved elimination area is. If any of the waste dirties his fur, wash it off. Clean his crate thoroughly before recrating him. Praise him for being clean. Stay diligent about normal housetraining routines until he regains his preference for a clean den. Even old Poms can learn new toilet tricks.

and react by promptly taking him out.

Accidents Happen

Despite your vigilance, there will be times when your puppy will have an accident in the house. You can catch him in the act if you are supervising him. First, interrupt him by startling him. Use a phrase like, "not inside" or "outside," and immediately scoop him up even if he is still going. Set him down in his toilet spot where he can finish the job he started and urge him to "go potty outside."

Back indoors at the accident site, do not ever, under any circumstances, scold your puppy, hit him, or rub his nose in the mess. This is punishment, not training, and he will learn nothing from your reaction. Instead, return him to his crate as soon as you bring him back inside, then thoroughly clean the spot. It is important that your dog understands that it is not his elimination which is the problem, rather the location indoors of the elimination that is inappropriate. The papers or rag with which you blot up the urine can be placed in his outdoor toilet area so he understands that this is where he is supposed to eliminate. Smelling his urine in his potty area and telling him, "good spot," can help reinforce the idea that emptying his bladder outside is good behavior which earns him rewards.

Going for a walk is a great reward to give your pup once he has eliminated in the appropriate spot soon after you've taken him outside.

With his keen canine nose, your Pom may be able to detect a lingering odor of urine even though you have cleaned the spot where he eliminated. Smelling this odor may cause him to think he should urinate there again. It may be possible to teach your dog that this is not correct behavior by telling him, "bad spot," and moving him away from the area and into another activity. Regardless, clean the spot again with a product that eliminates the odor of urine, and keep pursuing your dog's housetraining.

On occasion, uncontrollable events like severe weather, illness, or injury may interrupt your dog's routine. For example, some Pomeranians will refuse to go out to potty if it's raining. Or some owners may live in high rise buildings, and taking a puppy or dog out at frequent intervals may be difficult, time-consuming, or inconvenient. Because of their small size, it is possible in these circumstances to provide your Pomeranian with alternate potty options. High-rise dwellers can place a sod box on a balcony or patio. Poms can also be taught to use a litterbox. And puppy pads or newspapers can be laid on the bathroom, basement, or garage floor for special circumstances. Teach your dog to use these alternate facilities using the same techniques as for outdoor potty training.

Cleaning Up After an Accident—Carpet

In order to prevent your Pom from repeatedly urinating on the same spot on the carpet, it is necessary to get the urine and all of the odor out of the carpet and probably the pad underneath, as well. Here are some simple steps to follow:

- Suction up urine with a handheld wet-vac, or blot it thoroughly with newspapers and paper towels weighted down onto the urine-soaked area.. If using papers to blot, you may need to change the papers several times.

- After soaking up as much urine as possible, apply an enzyme cleaner specifically manufactured to remove all traces of the remaining odor. These products work by breaking down the protein in the urine. Follow manufacturer's instructions, then blot up any excess product.

- The spot can be washed with cool water and a pet-specific carpet cleaning chemical if needed. Follow product instructions and remove excess liquid.

- Let dry before allowing your dog near the spot. If he still smells the area with interest, repeat the procedure above until no odor remains.

- In some instances, urine may soak through to the pad. Carpeting may need to be peeled back to reach the pad for cleaning or replacement. Although less likely with a toy-size dog, it is possible that, if carpeting is repeatedly saturated in the same area, the urine may penetrate through the pad and into the wood of the subfloor. If this happens, it will probably be necessary to remove the old carpet and pad, replace the affected subfloor boards, and reinstall new flooring to remove noticeable odor.

Housetraining an Adult

When adopting an adult dog who has come from a shelter or rescue group, it is likely that he might not be housetrained or may have forgotten his housetraining. With these dogs, it is necessary to go back to the beginning and start with step one, exactly as you would with a puppy. Although adult dogs are usually capable of holding their urine longer than a puppy, there may be concurrent health problems which will necessitate going out just as often.

Keep in mind that small dogs in general and Pomeranians in particular may present more of a challenge to housetrain to total reliability. Breeders and rescue volunteers rate them as moderately difficult to housetrain.

"As puppies, they are usually easy to housetrain, or if you just have one [adult] dog," note Mary Jane and Dan Coss, rescue volunteers and Pomeranian owners from Ohio. "But with some rescues, older dogs, or multiple Poms at the same time, it may be almost impossible to housetrain them completely."

Intact males, particularly those who have been used for breeding, have a strong urge to mark by urinating on items in their territory. Indoors this includes furniture and carpeting. Unspayed females may also have a greater inclination to urinate indoors. The Cosses try to impress the importance of spaying and neutering, partly as an aid to housetraining. "Males should be neutered as soon as they start lifting their leg to urinate," they suggest, "By then, they want to mark and are nearly impossible to housetrain if they are not neutered."

Regardless of the circumstances, remember that faithful adherence to housetraining routines are essential if your dog is going to become—and remain—the clean, well-behaved, indoor companion he was bred to be.

LEASH (LEAD) TRAINING

Walking with your dog should be a pleasure. But as soon as some puppies feel that first tug from a leash, they resist. A few may even lay down or make sounds that closely resemble a "scream." However your pup reacts, before you and he can go for a walk together, he needs to be leash trained.

Since Poms may be prone to tracheal (throat) problems, hooking a leash to a neck collar may not be the best option. A harness that is loose enough not to tangle fur but tight enough that your dog can't slip out of it is a good choice.

Poms who are larger than average in size may do all right with a flat, nylon collar that has a break-away buckle, but ask your veterinarian's advice about which is best for your dog. Select a size that is slightly larger than your puppy's neck and adjust it so that you can easily slip two to three fingers beneath it when fastened. Make certain to adjust it as your puppy grows.

A few dogs will scratch or attempt to bite at a harness or collar when you first put it on them, but most adapt to it. Because many owners do not keep a collar or harness on their Pom all the time to prevent the fur from becoming matted, it may take a little training to get your dog to accept having something around his chest or neck. When he learns that the harness is associated with the pleasure of going for a walk, he should quickly get used to wearing it.

Choose a leash that is long enough to easily reach your Pom's short level without forcing him to stretch or pull. The material should be durable without too much weight, and the handle should be comfortable for you to hold.

To get your puppy used to being on lead, work with him indoors first. Let him smell the leash before clipping it to his

One of the reasons Poms seem to be more difficult to housetrain than some other breeds is because they're just so darn cute it can be easy to overlook mistakes.

Pomeranian Potty Problems

Why are Pomeranians more difficult to housetrain than some other breeds?

- Because they're cute. It's hard to make that precious pouf of fur go out in the rain if he doesn't want to go.

- Because they give you the cute look. It's easier to overlook mishaps when they look at you with those sweet, smiling faces than it is to enforce proper behavior.

- Because they're small. It's fairly easy to hide an indoor potty area if you're Pomeranian-sized, and much harder for a large human to find all those spots when they're under a bed or in the back of a closet.

- Because housetraining takes more time and a longer consistent effort than any other basic household training.

- Because some Poms, male or female, have a strong instinct to mark territory.

- Sometimes health problems may factor into the housetraining equation. Conditions that can cause a dog to relieve himself indoors frequently or suddenly may include bladder infection, diabetes, heart disease, kidney disease, certain medications, special diets, hypothyroidism, Cushing syndrome, inflammatory bowel disease, pancreatitis, parasite infestation, and more. Check with your veterinarian if your Pom has a change in bowel or bladder habits.

- Inappropriate urination or defecation can be related to separation anxiety, submissive urination, intense play, or upon greeting visitors. These types of mishaps tend to occur more frequently in younger dogs.

harness. Then let him drag the leash around behind him, while you supervise to make certain it does not get caught on the furniture. As he gets used to the presence of the leash, pick up the end and entice him with a treat to come while gently reeling him towards you.

Another technique teaches the puppy that you are connected to each other through the leash. Put his harness on him, then clip the leash to it. While holding the end, let your dog walk around and you follow him. Most dogs will respond with curiosity. Once you have his attention, show him a treat, then walk away from him while retaining hold of the leash. Use the treat to entice him to follow you. Praise him and offer treats as he follows you around.

Once your puppy is comfortable with the leash and harness, take him outside and repeat the process. If he is resistant, let him first wander to objects he wants to investigate, then teach him to go where you want him to go by coaxing him with a reward. Remember to praise him when he walks on lead under your control. Your Pom will learn that his leash is usually associated with pleasant activities.

TIME TO GET FORMAL

There is probably no better learning experience for your dog than that of a formal training class. It exposes him to a large variety of new dogs, people, sounds, smells, sights, and interesting situations. It stimulates his mind and intrigues his natural curiosity. By providing him with a framework that can show him how best to respond to these positive challenges, you are providing him with a guideline on how to cope with future challenges.

Obedience training is not a series of lessons that teach your dog to assume meaningless positions that you or he may never use in "real life." Formal training is an organized system that teaches your dog to respect your leadership and be obedient to your directions and commands.

Another important aspect of formal training is owner education. In class you can learn to better understand how your dog thinks. You'll learn how to set clear training goals for your dog and have him understand what you want. Class teaches you how to teach him, and how to effectively communicate with him – and he with you.

Outside of class, you and your dog will have a ready-made means for working on manners and proper behavior, both at home and in public. After you and he have attended classes, everything else you teach, whether it's just to be a good companion, or advanced training for competition or therapy work, will be built on the solid foundation you have laid.

Like dog breeds, dog training comes in many styles, from individual instructors teaching small groups, private trainers working with a single dog per lesson, to obedience training clubs that have several instructors on staff directing various sizes and levels of classes. Research your options to decide which type will work best for you and your Pom.

How to Find a Trainer

A good place to start searching for the right trainer is to ask dog-owning friends or neighbors with well-behaved dogs where they went for training. Were they happy with the instructor and the instruction methods? If not, why?

Ask your groomer and veterinarian for referrals. Look on bulletin boards in veterinary hospitals or pet supply stores for flyers and business cards posted by training clubs and private instructors. Check to see if your pet supply store, animal clinic, or even the local humane society offer training as part of their services. Watch for advertisements in the newspaper. Look in the yellow pages of the phonebook under, "Pet," or "Dog Training." Find out if a local social club, such as the YMCA or a community center, schedules obedience classes. Query a search engine on the internet for training resources in your area.

Once you have found a training group,

Cleaning Hard Surface Floors

It is much easier to clean up urine off any hard surface flooring than it is out of carpet. However, it is important to remove it quickly to prevent seepage into the grout of tile, between joints of wood, or beneath vinyl sheets. Prompt cleaning also prevents your Pom from smelling urine in an area where he should not relieve himself again. To clean, wipe up urine with paper towels or rags. Wash rags thoroughly. Next, wash the spot, using a cleaner specifically indicated for the floor type that is also safe for pets. Rinse with a damp cloth or moistened paper towels, then dry.

interview any potential instructors. Professional trainers do not have to be certified, but are the trainers in the group you're considering approved by any organization or board? If so, what requirements did they have to meet to become certified? How does their certification relate to their experience in training dogs?

Other important questions to ask include:

- What type of experience does a trainer have?
- How many years have they been involved in obedience with their own dog?
- How many years have they taught professionally?
- Are the instructors knowledgeable about dogs, and do they understand canine behavior?
- Are they up-to-date on recent developments in different training methods and techniques?
- Have any of the trainers ever worked with Pomeranians?
- Are they willing to assist you and your dog with your specific concerns?
- Are they willing to use the best training methods for your dog and not just a single style they have always used? If the instructor uses force-into-position techniques and punishment style corrections, it is probably not the best class for a Pomeranian.

The trainer with whom you choose to work should have the best interests of your Pomeranian in mind at all times.

- Can you schedule a time to observe a class? If an instructor is reluctant to grant permission, take this as a possible warning sign that something may be amiss and look for another resource.
- Is there a plan for the session and a goal for the course?
- Are the instructions focused and understandable?
- Do the trainers like the dogs and people with whom they are working?
- Are their methods positive and correct actions rewarded with praise?
- Are the dogs happy and relaxed or they apprehensive and confused?
- Are the people and dogs learning?
- Are the fees reasonable or worth the cost?
- Bottom line, can you and your dog train—and learn—with these instructors in the offered environment?

Types of Training

Which training methods an instructor uses is another, major criterion when selecting an obedience class; will the techniques work for your Pom? With so many different ways to train, the average owner can become confused trying to understand how each method works when making a decision.

Understanding what type of training and outcome you seek, and how far you want to go with the training is the first step. Manners, or behavior training, makes your dog an obedient companion at home or in public. Activity training is geared towards teaching your dog how to compete in specific events or work such as conformation, therapy, agility, dance, flyball, or to perform a specific service, and so forth. Basic obedience is nearly always a prerequisite before enrollment in training classes for any specific activity.

Smart and sensitive as they are, Poms usually respond best to positively based lure/ reward training methods.

Obedience training begins the use of more formal commands such as "sit" and "stay." It serves many purposes, including facilitating manners training, and offers varying levels of difficulty, but the focus is on the dog's response—how quickly and how well he responds to the commands. Classes teach standard commands that have been around for decades.

Many teaching techniques have been developed over the years. These training methods can be divided into two categories: **compulsive**, where the dog is forced to learn behavior; and **inducive,** where the dog is persuaded to learn the behavior.

Older methods tend to use force and punishment, and can include heavy-handed correction, coercion, discipline, stern tones, and harsh handling. These methods are currently out of favor except with the most difficult or aggressive of dogs. Considered inhumane by some instructors, they are not the method of choice for the tiny, soft-spirited Pomeranian.

Lure Training

This is a method where an object favored by the dog, such as a toy or treat, is used to coax him into performing the desired behavior. The dog is taught to watch and follow the object, is told

what to do, then rewarded and praised when the requested response is received. The lure is phased out as training progresses, and praise becomes the reward. However, the toy or treat can then be given after the training session.

Play Training

A variation on lure training, the theory to this method proposes that before a dog will work for his person, dog and human must be able to play together. The dog learns to relax and play in settings other than his home or yard. Training moves forward to the standard commands working with a toy used in the play sessions as the lure.

Natural Training

This focuses on the instinctual behaviors that drive a dog, as well as on his emotions It is a technique that believes the use of treats, toys, compulsion, or punishment are all the wrong ways to teach a dog. "Correct" training, to get the dog to respond to commands, is based on comprehending the innate nature of canines by learning how to communicate and work with them in a way which they truly understand. Praise and correction are given by vocal instruction, touch, and body language. The development of a cooperative human-animal relationship is central to this type training.

Positive Motivation

This is reward-based training that uses neither compulsion nor punishment. Corrections are only given in a positive, instructive manner so that the dog knows what you expect. Incorrect responses are ignored, and the dog is redirected toward the correct behavior with no emotional reaction. When he responds correctly, he is rewarded with treats. To strongly reinforce a correct response, the dog is often given a "jackpot" of treats—several tasty tidbits—which communicates to him in an obvious manner that he has done very well.

Owners are taught to "build a history" of positive reinforcement with their Pom at home by rewarding him lavishly for good behavior. Bad behavior is thwarted by prevention. For example, don't give your Pom an old pair of socks to play with if you don't want him to chew up your good ones. In class, dogs are trained on flat collars only (a must for Pomeranians anyway), using a regular versus special leash, and are given a surplus of praise, petting, toys, food, and play. Lures or clickers are often employed with positive motivation training.

Clicker Training

This is a more involved form of training that was originally used to teach large marine animals performance tricks. In recent years it has been utilized to train dogs, and this now very popular method has had quite a bit of success.

Traditional training methods use verbal praise as both a reward and a motivational reinforcer of correct responses. Clicker training breaks this tool into two components so that the click clarifies for the dog exactly which behavior earned him a reward, thus allowing him to understand precisely what response is expected from him when the command is given again in the future. This is known as "shaping behavior" and is a relatively new technique in the psychology tool box of training.

The click is the distinct sign that indicates to the dog the precise moment he responded correctly. If your dog is across the room from you and you can't give him a treat when he responds correctly to a command, he can still learn that the click means he will soon get a reward, thus motivating him to respond while also enforcing the likelihood of correct performance down the road.

Clickers can also be used with dogs who can't work for food rewards because they become overly excited, or for those few Poms who may not be motivated by food. The dog will still learn that the click is identified as a positive response.

Clickers work as a "secondary reinforcer." A "primary reinforcer" is the reward—a treat, a toy, or being petted—for which a dog is motivated to work. A secondary reinforcer becomes associated in your dog's mind with these rewards. An example of primary and secondary reinforcers in real life, would be picking up your car keys and jangling them where your dog can hear the noise. Your dog, in anticipation of a car ride, happily runs for the door. In this situation, the primary reinforcer is the ride and the pleasure it brings, and the keys, which are associated with the car outing, are the secondary reinforcer.

Poms are sensitive to food and body language, and there are many ways to combine these tools to get your pup's attention.

A clicker isn't the only means of attaining the advantages of behavior-shaping training methods. Any unusual, distinct sound your dog does not hear in other situations, such as a tongue cluck, trill, or pop, will work. A special reinforcer word may also be substituted for the click. The key to success is that the signal must come quickly and at the precise moment your dog responds correctly. For many trainers, however, the clicker tool is still considered easier to use.

Clicker training is a more involved technique than what many novices are ready to use. If you want to give it a try with your dog, it's wise to register for a training class where the instructor can teach you the proper use of the clicker. The advantages of clicker training are many—immediate feedback, clear identification of proper behaviors, association of the training work with rewards, and positive motivation.

Whichever type of training you choose as best for your Pom, faithfully commit to the endeavor. Your dog's behavior and emotional well-being depends a great deal upon a foundation of good training. Whether it's household manners or formal training, remember that dogs are constantly learning. Talk to them. Explain to them, without droning on and on, what you expect of them. By communicating to your dog, you will learn to understand him and he will learn to listen to and respect you, and will look to you for guidance in other matters of behavior. Teach him well, teach him throughout his lifetime.

Training Time

Length of home practice sessions should vary based on each individual dog's attention span and the purpose of your training. The Pom may get the most out of a lesson if training sessions are kept short enough to prevent boredom from repetition.

Most formal dog obedience classes last about 60 to 90 minutes, and instructors recommend that owners practice at home at least two or three times a week between classes. At home, after about 15 or 30 minutes, watch your dog for signs that his attention is drifting—wandering gaze, wandering off, sloppy performance—and be ready to quit on a positive note, with a command successfully completed.

If you are training for formal competition, then more frequent and longer practice sessions may be necessary. However, if your Pom still gets bored with this routine, try breaking lengthier training sessions into shorter ones: instead of working one hour, try two, half-hour sessions during the day.

BASIC OBEDIENCE

A good place to start with formal teaching is with basic obedience. Basic obedience is a series of six commands commonly taught in the majority of formal training classes. These commands—sit, down, come, stand, stay, and heel—are the foundation for not only all sporting or competitive canine activities, but also the platform for good behavior overall.

Pomeranians tend to be independent, free-spirited little dogs who like to make their own decisions about what they want

to do and when they want to do it. Some people may believe this means Poms are stubborn and hard to train. Despite this attitude, most Poms prefer to please their people and can be trained to respond to basic obedience commands. However, training should not comprise harsh or punitive measures that can easily crush the sensitive Pom's feelings, or even injure their small bodies.

Which training techniques works best with Poms? "Food!," says McClatchey. "It's very seldom you'll find one that is not food motivated. Poms can work for praise if food comes reasonably soon after the praise."

What doesn't work is physical force and harshness. "Coercion-style training works less with Pomeranians than with some other breeds," McClatchey explains. "If you have to correct a Pom, it shouldn't be an in-your-face kind of correction that will turn the dog off to training for weeks." Instead, she suggests getting the dog's attention in a firm—but not harsh—manner. Tell him that what he did was not the correct response. McClatchey also advises against using a "choke" or chain-linked type training collar because of the breed's possible problems with collapsing tracheas.

If your Pom is resistant to learning the basic commands, analyze the situation and figure out how to get his attention. Maybe he needs more praise or a method of learning that intrigues his bright and curious mind. "Many dogs learn best if you use both a verbal and hand signal right from the beginning," says McClatchey, "Since Poms are sensitive to body language, this gives them an additional clue. Just be consistent in the way you use your hand and body each time you give the signal."

If you are about to embark on a formal training adventure, these guidelines can prove useful for teaching your Pomeranian. Regardless of the method, teach yourself, the owner, first how to train your dog. Ask your instructor to show you the best way to accomplish this task, through modeling, rewards, praise, and the correct use of tools and signals.

Training Treats

A key to the successful use of treats as a reward is to offer soft, small tidbits that can be eaten quickly. Hard, crunchy, or large treats—like bone-shaped cookies or baby carrots—take too long to chew. Good options include semi-moist treats, niblets of cheese, or dried, cooked liver. If your Pom is on a special diet, check with your veterinarian about which treats are safe for him.

Sit

Hold a treat just above your dog's head and slowly move it backwards and slightly downwards. As his eyes follow the treat, he will usually sit. If he backs up instead, you may need to guide him by either gently using your other hand to slide down his derriere or to curve under his back legs and place him into a sitting position.

Sit is a fairly easy request for Poms to master. Once learned, it should be practiced in all sorts of places and under different circumstances.

Sitting on the floor with your dog may also help him to get the idea more quickly the first couple of times you try this.

When he sits, say, "good boy, good sit" with enthusiasm and give him the treat. Practice this until he understands that "sit" equals a reward, and he can respond without you on the floor or with a treat over his head. As training progresses, you will eventually teach your dog to learn to sit beside you when you come to a stop during a walk.

Down

You can begin training this command from a successful sit since your dog will already be halfway in position. A dominant dog may not like being in a down posture as he can interpret it as a signal of submission. But with enough positive reinforcement, he will learn it is an acceptable and praised response. Later in training he will also learn to assume "down" from a standing position.

With your Pom in a "sit," take a treat and slowly lower it to the ground in front of his feet while saying, "down." If your dog doesn't drop to the floor to get the treat, lay your other hand, without applying pressure, on his mid-back to indicate that he should not rise or stand. As he starts to crouch, move the treat forward and lower where he will need to slide into a full down position to reach it. It may help to bend over beside or kneel next to your dog to accomplish this.

When he is down, say "good boy, good down" and give him the treat. While he is first learning the command, do not ask him to remain in the position very long. As he gets used to being in a "down," he can be released after a longer hold, and eventually he will learn to execute a "down" as you stand beside him while he lies on the floor or ground.

When you want your dog to lie quietly for an extended period of time, such as at the vet's or while you are completing a task, "down" can be a useful command, as well as a more comfortable position for your Pom than "sit."

Heel

This is the one command that might prevent damage to your

dog's neck and your hand, and make daily walks more pleasurable for both you and your dog. To teach your dog to heel, start by having him sit at your left side. Take a step, always starting with your left foot, which is a signal to your dog that you are going to walk and he should come with you. Say "heel" and begin walking.

If your Pom isn't curious enough to get up and get going with you, or if he lags behind, coax him along by holding a treat near the position where you want him to walk beside you. If he tugs on the leash or rushes in front of you, don't let him drag you along. Gently shorten the hold you have on his leash as you keep walking. Repeat the heel command and slip the leash behind your waist so that it is impossible for him to forge ahead. Be careful not to get the leash so close that you cause strain on your dog's neck, or that you risk stepping on him.

Tell your Pom, "good heel," as he walks by your side in proper position. With practice you will be able to reduce your repetition of the verbal command and to allow the leash to hang loosely in it's proper position at your side.

Although it is easy to carry your Pomeranian, it is nevertheless important that he learn to walk in harmony with you. Despite his small stature, your Pom is still a dog and needs to walk for his own well-being. For your well-being, he needs to learn to walk beside you in heel.

Stay

The "stay" command is nearly always used with "sit" or "down," and sometimes the "stand" command. Early in training, your dog may be learning to stay more readily from the sit position, particularly if "down" is not his best command.

Begin with your dog sitting at your left side. In a firm, voice, that goes down in pitch (think of the sound that a motor makes as it winds down and stops), while saying the word "stay," move your arm with open hand, palm towards dog,

This Pom is being taught to "down" by being lured into position and rewarded with the treat when he is fully down.

from your left leg outwards about 45 degrees. Step deliberately but slowly away from your dog starting with your right foot, instead of the left used to begin heel. Using the opposite foot becomes a cue to your dog that he should remain where he is while you leave. Take a

Teaching stay is done by increasing the time of the request as well as the distance away from the dog.

couple steps, then turn and stand in front of your dog. After a very few seconds, return to your dog's side and praise him, "good stay, good boy."

If your dog gets up, get his attention with a sound like "eh, eh" ("no" or "bad" are too strong) and guide him back into position. When first training, you can repeat the command and hand signal until he understands what you want. You may also try standing on his leash with your left foot but be very careful not to apply any pressure to his harness or collar. Gradually reduce, then eliminate constant or multiple use of the command and hand signal as he learns to stay.

As your dog gains acceptance, increase the distance you walk away from him as well as the time you ask him to remain in his position. Stay should be taught in small increments, only moving to greater times and distances away, after your dog responds correctly to smaller demands. For competition, the goal in training stay is for you to be able to leave the room for two or three minutes while your dog waits for you either in a sit or down. In normal, daily life stay can be used to get your dog to hold a position as long as is needed, for example, when he's being groomed or receiving veterinary attention.

Come

Possibly the most important command your dog can learn is to come to you when you call. Should he ever get away from you, it is a command that may save his life. The key to success is to make your Pom *want* to come to you all the time. To achieve this, never call him to come, then correct him, punish him, reprimand him, or do something to him that he doesn't like. If you do, he will learn to always associate coming with being angry, fearful, or in discomfort, and he will more likely learn to run in the opposite direction. Instead, when he does come to you always offer praise.

Begin teaching "come" with your dog on leash. As you are walking, reel a long leash out until it is loose, then reverse your direction (without turning around) by moving briskly backwards. As you walk, call him to "come, come, come" in a happy, high-pitched, excited voice. As your dog comes toward you, gather the leash into your hand so that he can't run on past. Praise him, "good come," and give him a favorite treat.

Add the "sit" command to your routine, having him sit in front of you, then ask him to "come" as he gains more understanding of what you want and responds correctly. When you are unable to enforce the command, avoid calling your dog, especially while he is still learning. A good way to reinforce the come command and associate it with a positive event, is to use it when you call your dog for a meal, "Pom, puppy, come get your dinner."

Stand

Place your Pom in a sit-stay to start teaching the stand command, then turn and face his right side. With your right hand, hold a treat close to his nose, and while saying "stand," move the treat slightly up and away from his face. As he gets up and begins to lean towards the treat, but before he can take a step, slide your left hand under his belly towards his back legs and say "good stand, good boy." Do not use your arm to force him into a stand, just as a guide to help your dog find the position you want him to assume. Work towards teaching your Pom to stand and stay. This command is also useful for veterinary exams or grooming sessions.

It is a pleasure to have a Pom who stands and stays on request.

CONSISTENTLY CLEAR

Once your dog has learned the basic obedience commands, training does not have to stop. You and he can consider going on as a team to participate in various activities or competitions (more in Chapter 7). You can also use your training foundation to teach your Pom to perform tricks he enjoys that may amuse visitors to your home, or patients in a nursing home.

Pomeranians love being the star of any show, and this is one way to provide your dog with an outlet for his natural talents.

Whatever command or trick you teach, remember to break it

down into small increments, teaching him one step at a time. Always, always praise your dog when he responds correctly. Set specific and clear training goals, and plan how you are going to achieve them.

Involve the whole family, both in class and at home when practicing. Show each member of your household the commands your dog is being taught and which methods you are using to teach them. Be consistent in your approach, and be patient. Learning takes time.

Precisely communicate what it is you want your dog to do. Do not mix commands. For example, asking your dog to "come on and sit down," will only prevent him from understanding what you want him to do. Are you telling him to come, sit, or lie down? Use the correct command for each situation. Telling your Pom "down" when you really mean "off" will confuse him so that he does not know which response you want when. Select specific words or phrases to use when praising, correcting, or training and always use them. And when asking your dog to do something, remember that commands are statements, not questions, and are not optional requests but required responses. Be firm but not harsh.

Never yell at or smack your Pomeranian as part of training, and don't train when you are frustrated or angry. "It's important to never train when you're feeling grumpy. If you're tense or unhappy, your dog won't learn anything," recommends McClatchey, "If you feel yourself getting tense, give your dog a command to which he responds perfectly, then give him plenty of food and praise and quit for the day. Always quit training while you are ahead."

Whether it's training for competition or fun, the relationship that develops through training will provide you and your dog the opportunity to spend quality time together and allow the two of you to work together as a team in most any situation.

PROBLEM BEHAVIORS

To an inexperienced or uninformed person, canine behavior

More Useful Commands

Wait. Teaches your dog to wait at the door, or before getting out of the car, while you get his leash, etc.; can prevent bolting behavior, teaches patience.

Leave it. Teaches your dog not to pick up items that you don't want him to have; can prevent him from chewing or eating dangerous objects, spoiled food on the ground, dropped laundry.

Drop it. Teaches your dog to drop an item already in his mouth which he shouldn't have when you cannot reach him.

Give. Teaches your dog to hand you either an object which he already has but shouldn't, or to allow you to take away a toy with which you want him to finish.

Off or out. Handy for getting your dog off or out of places where he doesn't belong or that might be unsafe for him.

Enough. Indicates that the activity in which your dog is engaged is not bad, but it has limits, such as inappropriate timing or duration. When it's time for him to quit doing something, enough tells him to stop.

If you're uncertain how to teach these additional commands to your Pom, ask your trainer for assistance.

can be puzzling. Sometimes it's funny or cute, but other times we humans may see it as disastrous. Before you get upset with your Pom's behavior, you should understand that what may be unacceptable to you is perfectly normal for your dog. Learn how to determine if his behavior only needs redirecting so he can live in harmony with you, or if the behavior is abnormal and requires the intervention of a professional.

Normal Behavior
- Mouthing, chewing, or vocalizing during play.
- Cautious but curious.
- Active, energetic; short attention span while playing, especially puppies.
- Avoids direct eye contact until you have taught him to look at your face.
- Plays by pawing, batting at, or pouncing on toys, other pets, or people.
- Rolls over on back.
- Wants to be with you, follows you, or wants to lay against you.

"Abnormal" Behavior
- Biting, snapping, or attempting to bite; growling or aggression towards people or other pets; makes and maintains eye contact in an intimidating manner; possessive of food, toys or bed.
- Overly shy, timid, or fearful, wants to hide most of the time; frequent cowering or cringing; is agitated unless owner is present.
- Hyperactive, unable to concentrate or focus attention briefly.
- Continuous barking or crying.

   If your Pom is showing some of these "abnormal" behaviors, you should talk to your vet, trainer, or a behaviorist.

Your dog will quickly learn to associate the collar and leash with the pleasure of going for walks.

Aggression

Pomeranians seem to prefer the established order of their pack

Have some favorite toys on hand for your puppy so that should he try to nip, you can quickly replace your finger or hand with a toy or chew.

over meeting and making new animal friends. Given this preference, they may also tend to be a more dominant breed than some others. Dominance and aggression are not the same, but excessive dominance can sometimes cross the line into aggressive behavior.

Displays of aggression can include snarling, growling, lunging, snapping, biting, and can be triggered by many different things like perceived threats or invasion of space. Types of aggression can be fear aggression, territorial aggression, even dominance aggression, and more. Causes of the behavior are often difficult to determine, and expert help should be sought if your dog shows any signs of aggressive behavior.

Just because some Pomeranians are dominant does not mean they will be aggressive with other animals or in new situations. It just means that it's smart to keep a watchful eye on your dog when he's around other animals, meeting new people, or in an unusual situation for the first time. Not only is it safer for him, it also gives you the opportunity to interrupt the behavior if he begins to show signs of aggression.

First, study dog-to-dog communication so that you understand the difference between normal behavior and aggression. It's normal for dogs to communicate with each other about status and territory, so this communication should be permitted. Then, if you are uncertain whether or not your Pom is being aggressive, it is important to seek help. Aggression, even in Toy dogs, is an extremely serious problem

However, if your dog does show aggression towards another dog, person, or even you, tell him "no" and put him in his crate. Be cautious how you break up dogs who are fighting or how you handle a dog displaying aggression so that you do not get bitten. If the behavior continues, consult with your veterinarian. Referral to a behavior specialist may also be in order.

Biting, Snapping, and Nipping

Puppies love to play with their mouths and nip as part of this play. Between dogs, this is normal behavior, but it is behavior that needs to be discouraged when the nipping is directed towards a human. A dog must learn that it is unacceptable to intentionally use their teeth on a human.

When your puppy nips you, startle him with a loud "Ouch!" and move away from him, terminating the play in which you were engaged. This is similar to what his mother and littermates would do and is a signal to him to stop rough play. It is referred to as teaching "bite inhibition."

Substituting a toy may also redirect his desire to nip. If your dog continues to nip as part of play, add a firm "no bite" command and stop playtime by putting him in his crate. He will soon get the message that when he nips, his fun comes to an end.

Occasionally, if a puppy's nipping is ignored, and if the behavior is reinforced by the owner laughing at, accepting, or otherwise encouraging the dog to nip, nipping can sometimes develop into snapping and biting. This type of behavior is a difficult to reverse.

Snapping and biting are different from nipping. They have little to do with play and are primarily a display of dominance, aggression, or both. Snapping is usually a preliminary step that may lead to biting. It must be curbed by preventing the behavior from developing further. If you haven't started training your Pom, now is the time to begin.

Dogs bite for many reasons—fear, self-defense, protection of property, territory, or food, as a reaction to sudden pain, as a message of displeasure, or because the dog is indicating he's in charge. Often these reasons can be described as a warning for the perceived offender to stop, or as an attempt to protect himself or his owner from a perceived threat.

In some instances, dogs that bite may have been removed from their mother too early as a puppy, thus failing to have learned proper bite inhibition. In other cases, the dog may have been allowed to learn that he is alpha and in charge. A tendency to bite can also be genetic, such as when a bad temperament is inherited from a relative. This is another reason why you should carefully research from where you plan to buy a puppy. Dogs with bad dispositions should never be bred in the first place. If caught early enough during puppyhood, it may be possible to train away from this behavior, but it will take an

Poms may sometimes display territorial aggression with each other or when greeting new people or animals. Keep a watchful eye on your dog if you suspect he may do this, and if the aggression seems to be escalating, consult a professional.

"Alpha" is the first letter in the Greek alphabet. Applied to dogs, the term refers to the "first" dog, or in other words, the leader of the pack. Dogs thrive on order, so it is important that each member of their group—the pack—has his own, determined position, such as alpha, or leader. Ranking within a pack determines which dog eats first, gets the first choice of the best bed or toys, and so forth. Having pack hierarchy that is understood and accepted reduces the chances of fighting over such choices every day, since each member knows his place and rights.

Pack rank is still important to a Pom even when he is the only dog in the house. In his eyes, you and anyone else living in your home are members of his pack. No matter how clever he is, no dog should ever be allowed to run the household, so as the human responsible for your dog's care, it is up to you be the alpha.

educated, dedicated, and ever vigilant owner to prevent the biting from developing into a serious problem.

A history of abuse, sometimes even of punitive-type training can cause an otherwise good-tempered dog to begin biting. These dogs too may be trained away from the behavior, but not always. Again, owners will need to put in extensive effort to reverse the behavior.

If your dog indicates, by warning signs such as growling or snapping, that he is about to bite, sternly tell him, "No bite." Remove any toy, treat, or activity that your dog might consider as a reward for this behavior, and put him into a sit-stay. Remember not to yell, hit, or use any type of physical discipline that could cause your dog to think he must protect himself or assert his pack status.

If your dog does bite, or if his behavior escalates into biting, get help. Have him checked by a veterinarian for an illness or injury that might be undetected, particularly if your Pom has never shown any inclination towards biting behavior before. Seek the instruction of a trainer who is experienced with biting problems in toy dogs and who can show you how to teach your dog that you are alpha and in charge, without making him feel threatened.

A dog who bites is not at fault. Except when there is an injury or disease that causes pain, usually a human is to blame when a dog has learned to bite. Regardless, dogs who bite are dangerous. They are a liability. And they are bad news for good dogs everywhere else. Because of the Pom's tiny size, some owners may not believe it is a serious problem when their dog bites. Even though it may be considered cute by some to see such a small dog act big and ferocious, being bitten by any dog is never cute.

Whatever the reason, biting is *never* acceptable. (A possible exception to this rule is if the dog is defending you or himself from an actual attacker.) Listen closely again: biting is never acceptable. A dog that bites is a stressed, miserable dog. Because the conclusion to an episode of biting is often tragic, don't ignore the warning signs or accept biting in your Pom. Early intervention is critical if the dog (and possibly your insurance coverage) is going to be saved. If your Pom bites, seek professional help and stop the behavior.

Excessive Barking

Just like humans, dogs like and need to talk, some more than others. Dogs do this by barking. Usually they bark because they have information which they wish to communicate to us. Pomeranians seem to have more information to communicate to their people than some other breeds.

In fact, excessive barking, often described as yappiness, may be the top complaint among problem behaviors in this breed. Rescue groups specializing in Pomeranians note that some of the dogs they receive have been given up by their owners because they couldn't tolerate all the barking.

Additionally, dogs who bark to excess may create problems for their owners. Neighbors who complain may report the problem to city or county officials, who in some cases may have the right to press charges against a Pom's owner. Fines may be imposed by a court, or in the worst cases, the dog may even be forcibly removed. Landlords who receive complaints from other tenants may resort to issuing ultimatums to owners of noisy Poms: either get rid of the dog or move out.

If neighbors complain that your dog barks while you aren't at home, this may be a symptom of separation anxiety. Although this is not a common problem in Poms, this type of barking needs to be handled differently.

Solutions

So what can you do if your Pom is one who barks, frequently, and for long periods of time? Removing the triggers to barking is not likely to work, since it is normal for dogs to bark in many situations. You cannot control every situation which triggers barking, such as when unannounced guests knock on your door. Instead, start with

Socialization

Dogs are social animals. Without social exposure they may develop serious behavioral problems. With social contact, they thrive. Even if your Pom prefers to limit his socializing to the company of his family, it is still important that he be properly socialized.

"Socialization" is a term you hear quite a bit in the dog world, but what does it mean? The dictionary defines it as "preparation for cooperative living." Without socialization, your dog will not know how to behave around people, other animals, or in public. He could also become fearful, timid, or overly protective.

To socialize your dog, you should expose him in a controlled and positive manner to a wide variety of people, animals, places, sounds, smells, and objects, and teach him how to respond correctly to changing situations. Socialization should begin when your Pom is young and continue throughout his life.

When approaching a new situation, explain to your dog, in short, precise words, where you are going and what he will be doing. Also tell him how you expect him to behave. Hearing your voice is soothing to him, and gives him a word or phrase to associate with specific situations—and their likely outcomes. This in turn allows him to learn what he can expect in the future.

Calmly introduce your dog to the new place or person. Act as if the new situation is routine. If your dog acts hyper, teach him to "settle." If he is fearful, avoid a reaction which he may interpret as praise and which will reinforce the behavior. Don't force him to investigate, but don't withdraw him immediately from the new situation.

Start slowly with little excursions, such as taking your Pom with you to the bank drive-through, or have a neighbor meet you at a park to walk your dog. Dogs that are well-socialized tend to be happier, well-balanced, and better-behaved dogs.

Putting your Poms in an environment that helps calm them can keep them from barking excessively.

training to control the behavior. A recent and novel development in bark-control training is to listen to what your dog has to tell you, then thank him for the message. If he continues to bark, tell him, "enough."

You can also teach your dog to bark. Why would you want to teach a noisy dog to bark? Because by training him to bark, you can also train him when to bark, when to stop barking, and when not to bark. The first step is to teach your dog to speak on command. When he barks, tell him, "good speak," or create a situation where he normally barks, issue the command, and reward him.

Next, work on turning off the barking. Tell him, "no bark" and place a finger over your lips, whispering, "sshhh." This should get his attention and when he responds, tell him, "good quiet," or "good sshhh." "Quiet" can actually be taught when your dog is not barking. Do this simply by telling him "good quiet" while he is being still. Clicker training can be combined with "quiet" training so that your dog understands the exact quiet behavior for which he is being rewarded.

Barking excessively outdoors may be more of a problem than indoor barking, both for your neighbors to endure and for you to control. It is okay to let your Pom bark once in a while at squirrels or children playing up the street. But you will have to determine when he has barked enough, and again, control the behavior.

The easiest way to do this is by bringing your dog indoors. Don't bring him in as punishment. Teach him to come in when you call him, then reward him when he comes. Keep him in until he calms down. Each time you bring him in when he barks too much, he will learn that he only gets to play outside when he is quiet. Couple this with the "quiet" command, and soon you will have a method for controlling excess barking outside.

In a few cases, owners may still have difficulty preventing their Poms from barking excessively. If this uncontrolled barking damages relations with neighbors or a landlord, or becomes unbearable for the owner, some owners may think about having their dogs debarked.

Debarking is a surgical procedure, performed under general

anesthesia, which alters the vocal chords and permanently renders the dog incapable of barking. There are different degrees of debarking, ranging from a muffled bark to a barely discernible squeak. Veterinarians remind owners considering this surgery that it will not make the dog silent—he will still continue to vocalize, and some level of sound always remains.

Although no greater number of post-surgical complications in Pomeranians than in other breeds are reported by veterinarians, a few owners feel that their debarked Poms have had additional problems with their tracheas (an issue for the breed, anyway), such as scar tissue, which result in difficulty swallowing and breathing.

A large number of dog enthusiasts believe that debarking is cruel and inhumane and should never be performed on any dog. If bark-control training is not completely successful, other tools, such as a collar that issues a strong-smelling puff of citronella each time the dog barks, should be tried first instead. Once all other training methods have been tried for a sufficient period to determine they are not working, and all options have been exhausted but your Pom still barks excessively, *and* if this barking is creating *serious* problems which will result in the loss of your home or your dog's life, then you may wish to consult with your veterinarian about whether or not debarking can save the situation. But a word of warning—remember that debarking is permanent and disabling, and is a drastic option of last resort, to be done only if it will prevent your dog from losing his life or you from losing your home.

Whatever your Pom's reason for barking, listen, tell him when enough is enough, and teach him to be a good, quiet canine neighbor.

Chewing

Although Pomeranians aren't more prone to chewing than any other breed, like any other dog they do like to mouth and they like to chew, particularly as puppies. Chewing on a safe toy is fine, but chewing on your shoes or the furniture is not. The solution to destructive chewing is simple: prevent, supervise, and redirect.

Their strong desire to communicate can lead Pomeranians to bark excessively. Learning to channel that energy into appropriate behavior is part of the training your Pom needs if he develops this habit.

Teaching your Pom to sit up and wave is a good way to keep him from jumping up while still giving him the attention he craves.

While your puppy is out of his crate playing, watch him closely. If you are supervising his play time, he won't have the opportunity to chew on any items that are off-limits. An easy rule for chewing is that if it's on the floor, or within reach of your puppy, then it is okay for him to chew it. That means keeping shoes, remotes, pens, the kids' toys, or anything else that you don't want chewed, put away or shut out of reach from your pup. For large items that can't be removed, place a drop of Bitter Apple, vinegar or Tabasco sauce on the spot where your dog likes to chew.

Puppies need to chew, especially when they are teething, but adult dogs also need to chew. To meet this need, always keep a supply of safe chew toys readily available for your Pom. When your puppy begins chewing on a non-chew item, use the "give" command and take it away from him. Praise him for allowing you to take the item, then immediately substitute a chew toy and tell him, "good boy" when he takes it.

Digging

Digging is an activity many dogs love and is instinctual behavior for others. Dogs dig for a variety of reasons: to have something to do; to pursue small prey like a chipmunk; to make a comfortable bed in which to lie; to get out of a fenced yard; to hide a prized possession; or to find a cooler or warmer place to lay on the ground. The most common reasons that a dog digs may be because it's fun or for reasons that humans may never guess.

Like other Nordic breeds, Pomeranians seem to enjoy an occasional digging expedition. Owners report that their Poms dig outdoors during play. Because of their size, extensive damage to the yard is unlikely to occur. But Poms also like to dig inside in bedding, carriers, mattresses, carpet, and more, probably for some of the same reasons they dig outside.

As long as your Pom is not damaging the lawn or furniture, there's probably no reason to stop this behavior. But if your Pom is a problem digger, you might want to offer him a single area where he should confine his digging. Outdoors, provide him with a sandbox that's filled with white, filtered sand, and toys. Indoors, place a pile of old sheets, towels or a blanket in his play or sleep area and let him dig to his heart's delight. Once you show him that digging is acceptable in these locations and that the box and toys are his, this will usually curb his tendency towards destructive digging elsewhere.

If your dog is digging to make a comfy spot to rest in the yard, another option is to place a waterproof bed for him on a deck or patio. If he's digging to escape, secure the bottom of the fence line. Any digging you want stopped, tell him, "no dig" when you catch him in the act, then redirect him to the permissible digging zone or to another fun activity. Offer praise when he responds.

Jumping Up

When you really love your dog, you probably also love it when he eagerly greets you at the door, jumping up for a kiss and hug.

Licking and smelling of the muzzle to greet a pack leader who's returning to the den is normal behavior in dogs. This mutual face-level gathering represents the bonding and functionality of the pack. When you return home, your dog is just acting on this important instinctual behavior. In order to reach the taller members of their pack, your Pom adapts his behavior by jumping up to greet you.

Not every visitor to your home will be happy when your dog flies into their face to say hello as they enter your door. And there may be times when jumping up creates problems for you, such as if you're wearing delicate clothing, carrying packages, or if you are feeling fragile. Plus, it is possible that your Pom could get injured if he jumps too high.

You must decide if your Pom is going to be allowed to greet you

You can redirect inappropriate chewing and digging in the yard by supplying a safe, enjoyable toy for your Pom.

by jumping up. If you want him to greet you calmly, with all four feet firmly planted on the floor, it will be necessary to teach him not to jump, then consistently stick to the rules. Being allowed to jump sometimes but not others can be quite confusing for your dog; how is he supposed to know when it's all right to jump on you and when it's not? If you want your dog to jump for you but not on visitors, this will require extra training.

To teach your Pomeranian not to jump, he will need to be familiar with the basic obedience commands "sit," "stay," plus the extra commands "wait," and "off." Go out the door, then come back in. When your dog jumps on you, say, "off, no jump," and firmly but carefully place him back onto the floor. Turn away from him and tell him to "sit" and "stay." When he responds, praise him then stoop to his level and allow him to greet you as exuberantly as he wishes from the sit position. Release him from his sit and continue your entry as you normally would.

Eventually switch the "sit/stay" to "wait," once he has learned not to jump. With "wait," your dog can continue standing or walking about while he awaits your greeting, and you don't have to remember to release him from a stay. The important message is that your Pom is still permitted to greet you with plenty of enthusiasm but without jumping up on you.

Behavior Specialists

Occasionally, a dog can develop a behavioral problem which cannot be helped with training.

Dogs are complex beings, and it's possible that even the most educated of owners won't have the right answer on how to resolve their dog's issues. If you are in over your head trying to solve your dog's bad or baffling behavior, it may be time to consult an animal behaviorist.

Behavior specialists are educated to understand canine body language, communication methods, pack structure, and much more. Some veterinarians may also be diplomates of the American College of Veterinary Behaviorists and certified by the Animal Behavior Society. Most behaviorists come from a background in psychology and are certified through the International Association of Animal Behavior Consultants.

If you live near a university with a veterinary college or a post-graduate college, or in a large, urban area, you may be able to find a behaviorist by looking in the yellow pages. You can also find a behaviorist by searching the internet, starting with the board of behaviorists' website at www.iaabc.org or ask your veterinarian to refer you to a qualified specialist.

A few professional trainers with extensive experience may be capable of providing you with a behavioral consultation. Be cautious if you go this route. Is the trainer truly qualified to help you with your dog's problem? Additionally, some behaviorists with psychology degrees may limit their practice to pet animals, but do this work without a certification in animal behavior. Again, some of these counselors may be able to help, but make certain that they are knowledgeable about canine psychology, and are able to translate this knowledge into a plan that resolves your dog's issue.

Ask a potential behaviorist about her credentials, a history of her professional experience, or even for references. When selecting a behaviorist, look for one who has experience with Toy dogs in general, and maybe Pomeranians specifically.

How can you tell if your dog needs a behaviorist? Any sudden or extreme change in behavior, or behavior that has been deteriorating gradually over a period of time might be an indication. Start with a thorough veterinary exam first, since nearly 20 percent of abnormal dog behaviors are a result of a medical problem.

Don't be afraid to seek help from a behavior specialist. It could be the difference that turns your Pomeranian into a happier dog.

Separation Anxiety

Owners want their dogs to bond with them, but can your dog become too dependent? Yes. Separation anxiety, as the name implies, means that your dog becomes overly anxious when you are separated from him. In other terms, it means he is overly dependent on you. Dependent means "necessary to have" and an overly dependent dog has a higher than normal need to always be near its human. Fortunately, separation anxiety is not a common problem among Pomeranians.

Is Separation Anxiety Developing?

Traits in your Pom that may mean separation anxiety is developing include:

- Excessive shyness.
- Fearful; easily stressed.
- Inability to adapt to change.
- Destructive when not occupied with owner.
- Lack of interest in playing by himself.

A dog who does suffer from separation anxiety is not just unhappy when apart from his owner, he is extremely agitated and profoundly distressed. Signs that a dog may have separation anxiety include panting, whining, pacing, drooling, occasionally vomiting, and inappropriate urination or defecation while the owner is gone. Additionally, a Pom may bark almost non-stop until his owner returns. In extreme cases, depression, loss of appetite, self-induced injury like lick granulomas (lesions caused by repetitive licking), excessive and destructive conduct such as the shredding of clothing, digging up flooring, and chewing or scratching doors may also develop.

Exact causes of separation anxiety are not clearly understood. Lack of socialization, genetic, and poor breeding, a history of neglect, puppies who have been taken from their mother too soon, dogs who receive an unhealthy amount of attention and always get their own way, or even owners who are excessively needy of their dog's company are all possible reasons.

The best way to deal with separation anxiety is to try and prevent it. Reduce the possibility of your Pom becoming too dependent on just one person by having different family members feed him. Ask a friend to take him for a walk around the neighborhood. When you have to be in another room away from your dog, instead of closing the door, put up a baby gate so that he can still see you. Obedience training in a class with other dogs and exposure to new people, places, and sounds, is one of the best ways to provide your dog with the confidence that can help prevent separation anxiety.

If your Pom shows signs of separation anxiety, desensitize him to your departures. Place your dog in his crate with a favorite toy, then go outside for a few minutes. When you come back inside, leave him in his crate for a moment. Repeat this procedure, gradually extending the amount of time you are out.

You may feel you know and understand your Poms, but when problems arise, you may not have the objectivity or experience to determine what is causing them.

Remove the clues that you are leaving—keep your keys in the garage, leave your coat in the car, park on the street instead of in the driveway. You can also act as if you're leaving, then don't. Put on your jacket, pick up your keys, walk towards the door, then turn around and sit down instead. Shortly, get up and put away your keys and jacket without leaving. And don't make a big fuss about departures and returns since they are a normal part of household routine to which your dog needs to adapt.

When you actually leave, turn on a radio and a light, place an item of clothing that smells like you in your dog's crate, and allow access to toys that will keep your Pom occupied until you return home. Although it doesn't work in all situations, another Pom to keep your dog company may also reduce his anxiety while you are away.

Submissive Urination

If your Pom piddles on the floor, or rolls over and dribbles urine on his belly whenever you come home or visitors enter your house, he is probably urinating submissively. This does not mean that your Pom's housetraining is not taking, or that he is misbehaving.

Submissive urination is a sign of respect to the alpha of a pack, given upon his return to the den. It may also occur at feeding time or other times when the dog feels the need to submit. Dogs that urinate in submission may also do so when they are excited, such as when they greet new people. This is more common in puppies and younger dogs. These dogs may not even be aware that they are urinating in these situations.

Generally, most dogs outgrow submissive or excitement urination. In the meantime, owners need to stick with their normal housetraining routine, clean up the puddle, and move on. It is best not to react at all to a dog that has urinated this way. If you yell, or otherwise react in a negative or emotional manner, the dog will perceive it as a threat, and feel the need to appease you by being even more submissive and urinate even more. The same holds true for excitement urination— yelling excites the dog and he continues to urinate.

If the problem continues, treat it by training. Give your dog confidence through praise and reward for obeying commands. Being able to respond to commands, such as a sit-stay, gives him another outlet for showing submission to you, the leader of the pack.

ADVANCED TRAINING
AND ACTIVITIES

With Your Pomeranian

Sitting at home, cuddling with your Pom, may not be enough activity for you or your furry friend. If you want to get active with your dog there are several options, such as sporting competitions or visits to the elderly. Most will require additional training, and a few are just for fun. All are a good way for both of you to bond and get more out of your time together. So what can you do with your Pom?

CANINE GOOD CITIZEN

Pomeranians are small—and portable—so they can easily travel about with their owners. Being trained and well-mannered is an essential prerequisite to such ventures. Earning a Canine Good Citizen (CGC) title is a way to offer proof of good behavior, particularly to non-dog persons and to businesses or motels that might be reluctant to admit a dog, otherwise.

CGC is an AKC program designed to recognize dogs who display good behavior at home and in public, and to emphasize responsible pet ownership to the community. Although begun in the United States, many European and Asian countries have similar programs.

Canine good citizenship is awarded to your dog based on the successful completion of a multiple-step test. Dogs must be presented in a certain manner and respond to several commands during the test, which is administered by certified evaluators. The commands include the following:

• **Accepting a friendly stranger.** With dog on leash, owner is greeted by the evaluator while on a simulated walk. Dog remains calm at owner's side while they chat, without approaching the evaluator.

• **Sitting politely for petting.** Dog sits at owner's side while evaluator pets him in a friendly manner. Dog must not shy away.

- **Appearance and grooming**. Dog is inspected by evaluator to ascertain that dog is clean, groomed, and healthy. Feet and ears are gently examined, and dog is brushed as part of the test. Handling and grooming must be accepted calmly.
- **Out for a walk.** Not as formal as in basic or competitive obedience, dog and owner must walk together and execute a right turn, left turn, about, and halt. Dog is to walk on a loose lead and pay attention to owner.
- **Walking through a crowd.** Dog and owner walk around and close to multiple people. Dog can show interest but should not be out of control, shy away from, or jump on people.
- **Sit, down, and stay.** On a 20-foot leash, dog does a "sit," and a "down." A "stay" will be requested from either position at the evaluator's discretion. Owner walks to end of leash, then returns, while dog remains in place.
- **Come when called.** With dog in a "stay," owner walks away from dog, then calls him to come.
- **Reaction to another dog.** With dog on leash, owner walks toward another individual also walking a leashed dog. While people talk, dog may only show casual interest in the other dog without leaving owner's side.
- **Reaction to distraction.** Evaluator chooses two distractions from a variety of actions—dropping large or noisy items, moving large items, joggers passing, and so forth. Dog may show interest, curiosity, or even seem mildly startled, but may not bark, run away, panic, or show aggression.
- **Supervised separation**. On leash, dog remains with evaluator while owner goes out of sight for three minutes. Dog does not have to stay in position. Mild nervousness or anxiety is acceptable, but barking, whining, or continual pacing are not.

Demonstrating good manners while walking on leash is expected from Poms taking the Canine Good Citizen test.

During testing, owners may talk to their dogs as needed to perform exercises, but treats are not allowed. Testing is done in a flat-buckle or slip collar and leash, and owner should bring his dog's own brush. Evaluators supply the remaining equipment and people.

Dogs will be disqualified if they eliminate during the test. Growling, snapping, biting, or displaying aggression towards people, animals, or test objects will also result in failure of the test. Dogs who pass the test receive a CGC certificate, and their new title is recorded with the AKC.

To prepare your dog for the test, he should be well-socialized and responsive to basic obedience commands. Tests are administered at many dog or breed events and competitions, through obedience clubs and therapy groups. To find an evaluator or an upcoming test in your area, contact the AKC or look on the AKC website.

OBEDIENCE

Did your Pom enjoy obedience classes? Did he pass the CGC test with flying colors? If so, then obedience at the competitive level may be an activity you want to pursue. Obedience trials were originated with the explicit purpose of demonstrating the ability of dogs to be good companions to humans.

In formal obedience competition, the commands learned in basic obedience training are constructed to test dog and handler on their ability to comprehend and execute these commands with precision. Dogs earn titles based on the completion of exceedingly more difficult tasks at each level of competition.

At a trial, competitors in the same class are all required to perform the same series of exercises. Judges grade the dog and handler according to a scale of points that deduct for flaws, refusals, and imprecise movements. To earn an AKC obedience title, dogs must have completed three successful trials (qualifying legs) with scores of no less than 170 points out of a possible 200.

Exercises in each class are dependent upon which title an owner is seeking for his dog. Beginner obedience starts with the six most common commands taught in basic training classes. Commands given by the judge increase in difficulty with each level of competition, including the addition of hurdles, long "down-stays" with owners out of the room, and finding articles covered with the handler's scent.

Titles that can be earned include the beginner's or Novice level and CD for Companion Dog. Next is the Open Class, where dogs can become a Companion Dog Excellent (CDX) by performing more of the competition commands off-leash. The most difficult levels are the Utility trials. Dogs who successfully complete, under three different judges, such exercises as commands given only by hand signals (silent

In higher levels of competitive obedience, Poms learn to retrieve and carry certain articles.

commands) and directed retrieving of a single specified article out of several, earn either the UD (Utility Dog) or UDX (Utility Dog Excellent). In addition to earning these titles, a dog may also be awarded a High in Trial (HIT) win, if his score is the highest for the day in his category.

At the very highest level of competition, dogs can go on to earn an Obedience Trial Championship (OTCH). This title is bestowed when dog and handler have earned 100 points by placing at least fourth or higher, under three different judges, in the Open and Utility classes. An OTCH is very difficult to obtain, usually earned by extraordinary dogs with owners who make training and competing for the title a major goal in their lives.

As strong-willed, independent thinkers, some Pomeranians may not be inclined towards obedience competition. However, because they are intelligent and want to please their people, Pomeranians can learn to compete—and earn titles—with the right training methods and plenty of practice.

If your Pom enjoyed and did well in basic obedience, it might prove satisfying for both of you to earn an obedience title or two. At national and regional Pomeranian specialty events, there are usually plenty of obedience Poms in competition, and many of them compete quite successfully.

If you want to see if earning an obedience title is fun for you and your Pom, "Take classes at local obedience clubs or training schools, then go to matches. Go to a dog show that has obedience and watch the competitions. If you are unfamiliar with the exercises, ask some of the competitors what they are doing," obedience instructor Wendy Donnelly sadvises. "It's well worth the effort to take your Pom into the formal obedience ring."

RALLY OBEDIENCE

Rally-O is similar to obedience, but at a more relaxed pace. The sport is designed to be more fun and a little easier for both dog and owner. Competitions are not as formal and do not require as much precision, although dogs must still understand and respond to various obedience and other commands.

Owners and dogs progress through a course that consists of multiple stations. These stations have signs which instruct the handler what command the dog is expected to perform next. The total amount of stations and complexity of the commands, which can include small jumps, are determined by the level of competition, and are based on the classes successfully completed in the past.

Handlers may talk to their dogs throughout the course to show them what actions they want them to perform, and hand signals may be given more than once for each command, unlike obedience. The sport promotes the use of encouragement and praise for the dog by his owner. Rally-O was designed to bridge the activity gap between completion of a CGC and formal obedience. Pomeranians who might not enjoy or respond well to the more rigid requirements of obedience may enjoy rally obedience better.

Because of the more relaxed requirements, physically challenged owners and dogs can easily participate. "Tuffy had an enlarged heart before he died, but he still wanted to work," Barbara McClatchey, UKC obedience trials and AKC rally-obedience judge, tells of her multi-titled Pomeranian, UUD Mar-Vic's Stuff'd Black Bear, UDX, RA, NA, NAJ, CGC, TDInc., HOF, GC. "The vet said to let him do what he wanted to do. He finished his advanced rally title before his death."

Rally-O is a sport that is new to the canine competition scene. Training classes and sanctioned trials are in the early stages, so you may have to hunt to find rally-o near your area. If you think you and your Pom might like to try this fun competition, check with the AKC or the Association of Pet Dog Trainers for seminars or events near your area.

AGILITY

Agility is high-action excitement and fun for dog and owner, and is probably the most popular sport in all of canine competition. Trials are run on a varying course of obstacles over which the handler must successfully direct his dog in a limited amount of time.

Obstacles include jumps, tunnels, ramps, teeter-totters, weave poles, elevated walks, A-frames, and more. Because agility is as much play as it is work, most dogs enjoy the sport immensely. The fast pace and audience

Make it a Game

"Make each exercise a game that is set up for your Pom to win. That makes it more enjoyable for him to work, and they continue to want to please you when you do this," says Wendy Donnelly, obedience instructor and owner of Tiny Tim Pendleton, a Pomeranian who has earned the Utility Dog title and believes obedience is a fun game. "Keep a good sense of humor because at times Poms act like clowns and will do anything to make their owners laugh. Laughter is their greatest reward."

enthusiasm create an atmosphere that is well-suited for the Pomeranian who loves to be the center of attention.

"I had seen dog agility on TV and was amazed. It was fun and exciting, so I investigated and found it wasn't just for big dogs. Little dogs were very much into agility, too," says Mandy V. Kiely, agility enthusiast and Pomeranian owner. "Honey Dew and I started training and she loved it, loved it, and showed signs of being a great agility dog."

Dogs that compete in agility should first have a solid foundation in basic obedience training and work well with their owners. Next, start out with beginner agility classes given by a good training school. Introduce each object slowly and have patience while working towards each goal or new obstacle. Reward successful performance with a treat and praise. Pomeranians are smart, attentive, good listeners, and watchers who wait to see what is next, all attributes that help make agility training much easier.

"Always have patience, make training fun and upbeat, end on a positive note, and don't overtrain," instructs Kiely. "An agility dog should be well-socialized, used to being around lots of barking dogs, noise,

Dog Sport Safety

Before engaging in any competition or strenuous activity with your dog, he should be thoroughly examined and cleared by a veterinarian. For the Pomeranian, this means paying particular attention to patellas that may luxate or a trachea susceptible to collapse. Vaccinations should be up to date (or antibody titres sufficiently high) so your dog is protected against the most serious communicable canine diseases.

If your dog is injured, sick, or showing early signs of any change in health, don't compete. At competitions, avoid getting too close to any other dogs who look or act as if they are ill. If your bitch is in season, you may not be permitted at some events. At those where she is allowed, keep her crated away from intact males! Teach your dog "no sniff" in regards to greeting other dogs, and enforce the no-smell zone.

Use the appropriate collar for the type of activity. The wrong collar or dangling ID tags may interfere with your dog's performance or cause an accident. Proper size collar and length of leash is also important to correct performance.

Slip-proof your dog. Trim the hair back, short, around his feet and foot pads, and cut his toenails. Mats are usually used to prevent slippage, but if the surface where he will be competing is slippery, apply a "sticky paw" product to the bottom of his feet which also helps prevent slipping.

When dogs are first learning above-ground obstacles, use a second person as a spotter to reduce the chance of falls.

Dress for the weather; leave an umbrella in your car or tack box. In hot weather, bring ice packs, extra water, and tarps or pop-up shelters for creating shade, maybe fans and extension cords, if electric is available. For cold temperatures, does your Pom need a sweater, or even booties if it's icy or extremely cold? Pack a blanket and extra towels. Keep a watchful eye on your dog if the weather is extreme.

Go to events prepared. Bring your dog's crate and bed. Pack plenty of bowls or paper plates for food, bottled water, dry food, treats, and plastic bags for cleaning up after your dog. Make sure you bring all the supplies you need to compete, like brushes, balls, costumes and so forth. Also pack an extra leash, proper ID, a first aid kit, and copies of medical records, or group credentials, if needed. A folding chair for down time is handy.

Always watch your dog. Keep him safe from large dogs, away from show equipment and supplies, and out from under the feet of quickly moving people. Let him relax and have fun, but don't let him misbehave.

Agility courses consits of obstacles like tunnels, A-Frames and jumps.

and the hustle and bustle of a dog show."

In addition to training, Kiely believes it is essential that the bond between you and your dog should be strong, that they trust you 100 percent. Also, if your Pom has knee problems like luxating patellas, it's probably best that he not participate in this physically demanding sport. But if your Pom is healthy and shows interest in running and jumping, give it a try.

Kiely notes that there are several ways to introduce your Pom to agility, such as coaxing him to run through a play tunnel. It is also possible to purchase agility equipment for home practice once you have some experience training with your dog. Kiely has an agility course set up in her yard where she and her two Poms train about three times each week.

Besides having fun, there are over two dozen titles to be earned by winning in agility, not only in AKC events, but also in those sponsored by the UKC, NADAC (North American Dog Agility Council), USDAA (United States Dog Agility Association), the KC, and others around the world. Each organization offers multiple levels of competition that increase in difficulty with every advance towards the next stage. The number and type of obstacles change as well.

"Honey Dew advanced through AKC Novice and Open to the Excellent level in just 10 months," exclaims Kiely, who loved agility so much she began competing with a second Pomeranian, Lilly Belle. She says they are working towards Honey Dew's MACH title (Master Agility Champion), one of the highest achievements in the sport.

A Pom and his person can have tremendous fun competing in agility. Just don't let it get too stressful. Remember that the activity is not primarily about winning, but about enjoying each other's company.

Flyball Organizations

If you think you and your Pom would like to compete in Flyball, see www.flyballdogs.org to find a nearby team or event, or contact the North American Flyball Association. Flyball organizations are also active in the U.K., Belgium, and Australia.

FLYBALL

Poms who love to run fast or catch balls may find this active sport perfect. Flyball is run as a relay race, with one team of dogs playing against another. Four dogs per team each take a turn racing across four hurdles towards a box where they must step on a spring which then releases a ball. The dog must catch the ball, reverse direction, and jump over the hurdles again on his way back to the starting line. As soon as he returns, another dog takes off, until all dogs have run the jumps and brought back a ball.

Teams compete in elimination heats until the last two teams have run and one them is the final winner. Height of the hurdles is based on the height of the shortest dog on the team, so fast Pomeranians can become coveted team members. The minimum jump height is set at 8 inches (20.3 cm) for shorter breeds like the Pom. Regardless of height, hurdles are spaced evenly apart over a distance of approximately 50 feet (15.2 m).

In addition to a team winning a flyball tournament, individual dogs may also earn titles based on a point system. Titles are Flyball Dog (FD) and FD Excellent (FDX), Flyball Dog Champion (FDCh), Flyball Dog Master (FM), FM Excellent (FMX) and FMX Champion, and for dogs with exceptional winning records, Flyball Grand Champion.

How can you tell if your Pom might enjoy flyball? A couple of signs are when he is crazy about catching a ball and loves to play fetch. He will also need plenty of drive to run and to get the ball. Personality is also important. Flyball dogs should be confident, well socialized, outgoing, and able to ignore noisy surroundings packed with lots of busy people and dogs.

Even if he's a natural at running, jumping, and catching, formal training will still be needed to get him ready for competition. In the recent past, training used to take about six months, but with current methods, plenty of classroom practice, and the use of manuals and videos, training from start to tournament can take as little as 12 weeks.

No special methods are usually required to teach a Pom, particularly if he is eager to play. Start by encouraging your Pom to catch and hold the ball, which can be slightly smaller to accommodate the Pom's tinier mouth. Take the training one segment at a time—jumping over hurdles, catching, retrieving, and so forth.

Handlers and spectators enjoy the competitions equally as much as the dogs do. Flyball provides a wonderful opportunity for you and your dog to play together.

FREESTYLE

Freestyle is dancing with dogs, a competitive or demonstrative event where owners and dogs perform choreographed moves to music. Steps are loosely based on obedience-style movements, such as heeling, and incorporate dance steps with a creative flair. Both handler and dog are in costumes that correspond with the theme of the music.

Barbara McClatchey, who also gives freestyle demonstrations with her dogs on therapy visits, says that Poms, hers included, enjoy the sport. "As soon as the music started, my dog marched his feet up and down, ready to go," she says. "He just loved to move to the music." Demonstrations are equally enjoyable to audiences, who are often awed by the dogs' performances.

Dogs and owners are judged on teamwork, style, creative artistry, athleticism, and interpretation. Freestyle is designed to demonstrate the joy of the human-dog bond while both owner and dog have a good time winning titles. For more information about dancing with your dog, contact one of the national freestyle organizations (listed in the reference section).

With their spirited and bouncy personalities, Pomeranians make natural "doggy dancing" partners. Try it with your Pom and you might get hooked.

CONFORMATION (SHOWING)

As the name suggests, conformation is an event where a dog is judged on how closely he conforms to the standard for his breed, in this case, to the standard for the Pomeranian. A dog is judged against a detailed standard for the purpose of evaluating which males and females are the best to pass along superior genes and continue their breed by producing puppies.

What Does it Take to Make a Show Dog?

Few dogs born are destined for the show ring. What are the extras that make up a show-quality dog, one bred to be in the winner's circle? A show dog:

- Conforms physically to a detailed description of what an ideal Pomeranian should be;
- Has been planned for generations before he was born, and has ancestors that are also show dogs;
- Is healthy and in excellent condition;
- Has an outgoing personality and is not nervous, fearful, or dull;
- Is trained and well-mannered;
- Has confidence, and clearly says, "Look at me—I'm special!";
- Is a beloved companion to his owner.

But a dog show is much more. It's also a beauty pageant, a muscle contest, and a beautiful sport for spectators to watch. Additionally, it's an activity for families and an event for socializing. And it can all be a bit confusing for those unfamiliar with the process.

Competition starts with experienced, educated judges who evaluate dogs in single breed classes divided by gender and age. Handlers pose dogs in a stand for inspection of their body structure and type, fur color and texture, correct eyes, head, tail, bite and ear-set, and even temperament. The handlers then "gait" the dogs around the ring, individually and as a group, in order to demonstrate the movement appropriate to the breed.

Winners are selected from each class, then the best male and female are chosen from these selections. These dogs, designated as Winners Dog and Winners Bitch, are awarded points based on the number of dogs they beat. Once a dog has earned a sufficient number of points, he becomes a "Champion of Record," which allows him to place the title "CH" in front of his name.

The Winners Dog, Winners Bitch, and dogs who have already earned their championship then compete for Best of Breed. Dogs chosen as Best of Breed, from every breed class, advance on to the Group class.

The Pomeranian, which is in the Toy Group, competes against the winning dogs from other breeds, such as the Pug or Pekingese, which are also in the same group. A winning dog from each group of breeds (seven in AKC and CKC, nine in KC) then goes on to compete for Best in Show—the dog who is judged to most closely conform to his breed's standard on that day.

"If someone is interested in showing, I recommend that they not buy a pup for about a year," suggests Carolyn Bonin of Rivendell Pomeranians. "During that year, they should read the Pomeranian magazines and books, and talk to exhibitors and breeders. Joining a local breed club is a good way to make contacts and learn. Novices should go to as many dog shows as they can and watch the Pomeranian judging."

So, long before a puppy is acquired, future show dog owners must research the breed's standard, breeders, advertisements, pedigrees, and health histories before selecting a show prospect and making a purchase. An owner who wishes to handle his/her own dog will perform better if he/she takes handling classes and learns proper ring techniques.

Before entering the ring, the future show dog needs training, as well. Handlers should start teaching a show prospect at a young age to accept being groomed, posed, and inspected, and being in noisy crowds around many dogs. Show dogs need optimal nutrition from day one and should be on a regular exercise program to build and maintain muscle. Plus, the high-maintenance coat of a show Pom needs to be kept in top condition at all times.

Not only must you have an exemplary dog and good handling skills, showing a dog in conformation requires a considerable commitment of time, money, and effort most days throughout the year. Why commit to such a monumental effort? Most successful, reputable breeders believe the best reason to show in conformation—and the only reason to ever breed puppies—is to improve the breed and to have a great time with your dog. Conformation focuses on the creation of healthy dogs that will make good companions generation after generation. And there is great satisfaction on a more personal level both from earning your dog's title and from the bond that develops between you and your dog while working together.

A Pomeranian who is competitive in the show ring must possess impeccable form and a winning personality.

If competing with your dog for honors in the conformation ring sounds like an activity you'd enjoy, research, study, watch, and learn everything you can about Pomeranians and dog shows from the experts. "Getting started in showing is tough.

Show dogs are taught from the time they're puppies to accept everything from being groomed to perfection to how to act in the ring.

Show quality is not always cut and dried. It takes time to develop an eye for a good Pom," says Bonin. "Ask a mentor or some other experienced person to help you."

Championships

To earn an AKC Champion title, a dog must beat other dogs in multiple age and gender classes to become Winners Dog or Bitch. Based on how many dogs are bested, up to a maximum of five points at one time are earned. Some of the points won must be "majors," where the dog earns three or more points in a single breed class. A total of 15 points, with two majors, are necessary to become a Champion of Record.

In the UK, a dog must win three Challenge Certificates (CC) from three different judges, with one of these Certificates awarded after the age of one year. To win a CC, a dog must already have been chosen for Best of Sex.

Earning the CC in the UK is not simple, as not all shows offer these certificates. CCs are allocated by the Kennel Club based on the popularity of the breeds being shown. Additionally, dogs which have already earned a CC can continue to compete for more certificates. It is not uncommon in KC shows for dogs who win frequently at the Breed, Group, and Best in Show levels to never become champions.

A Canadian championship is earned when a dog is awarded a total of 10 points by three different judges. One of these wins must be worth at least two points, given at either the Breed or Group level.

THERAPY DOGS

Therapy dogs are out-going, well-mannered dogs who, along with their owners, visit residents or patients in nursing homes, hospitals, and other in-care facilities, such as assisted living villages. Because these people may be cheered or comforted by the temporary companionship of a dog, the visits tend to improve the quality of life and health for

Conformation Eligibility

To compete in conformation, dogs must:
- Be registered with the AKC (or other relevant kennel club such as the CKC or KC);
- Not have any disqualifying faults as defined in the Pomeranian standard;
- Be a minimum age of 6 months;
- Be in mandated show trim;
- Not be spayed or neutered.

these persons through friendly contact with an animal that relieves depression, reduces stress, and promotes health.

Petting a Pomeranian a day can keep the blues away, according to their owners, so why not share some of that joy with others who are down, sick or institutionalized? With their adorable, smiling faces, and personalities that thrive on loving and making people happy, Pomeranians are ideal candidates for therapy dogs. Poms also make good therapy dogs because they are cuddly and small enough to easily sit with a person on a bed or in a wheelchair.

For those interested in doing therapy visits, it is necessary for owners to socialize their Pom to the types of sounds, equipment, furnishings, flooring surfaces, smells, and people they might encounter on institutional visits. A good foundation in basic obedience training is important. Dogs should be at least one year old and, certified and registered with a recognized therapy dog organization.

Qualification to become a Therapy Dog includes examination by a veterinarian to show that the dog is free of parasites and disease, and is current on vaccinations. A record of this exam is given to the certifying organization by submission of an annually completed health record form. Testing by a certified evaluator usually requires a canine candidate to pass the CGC test, along with tests designed to

evaluate reactions and behavior in an institutional setting. Besides the 10 CGC exercises, these additional evaluations judge reactions to medical equipment, the ability to respond to the "leave it" command, acceptance of obvious infirmities, and saying hello.

In some instances, passing tests to receive affiliation with a national organization may not always be necessary. Some Pomeranian owners who are active with therapy visitations join local or regional groups who sponsor therapy programs. However, these Poms must still be well-socialized, experienced in public (as is a show dog, for example), and owners must provide documentation from their veterinarian that indicates the dog is healthy and of stable temperament.

Their cute, cuddly, people-oriented personalities make Pomeranians exceptional therapy dogs.

Additionally, Poms who are going to be therapy dogs should be calm, enjoy meeting strangers, accept being handled by lots of

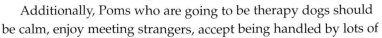

people, and adapt readily to unusual situations. Owners must also like meeting new people and should be good listeners, willing to talk with patients and residents while they pet the dog. Retired show dogs, already well-mannered and without a job, often make good therapy dogs.

Clothes for Competition

"Dress for success" isn't just a saying for business; it applies to competitive dog sports, as well. Wearing the proper attire can make your ring time easier and more effective.

Conformation. The most formal sport. Handlers should wear business dress: suits, matching or coordinated pant suits, or dresses, with plenty of pockets for bait and brushes. Choose colors that accent your dog's appearance, but don't stand out. Clothing should allow free movement for bending down to the dog and for gaiting, but without being sloppy. Shoes should be comfortable and made for running but also not have a too-casual appearance.

Obedience. Tailored casual, but with room for adequate movement. Competitors often wear jeans and other weekend style clothes, but overall appearance should make a neat impression. Shoes should be non-slip.

Agility. Similar to obedience but may be dressier. Handlers may wear matching outfits in some competitions. Khakis and golf shirts are popular. Clothes should fit loosely for running. Some participants wear tailored knits that stretch for movement, but return to a tighter fit when standing. Quality athletic shoes are essential.

Freestyle. A creative costume that is both entertaining and permits a large range of motion. Dog's costume should be safe while also permitting movement, but without causing him to stumble. Outfits should complement the theme of the music and dance.

Flyball. Casual, comfortable, and suited to athletic activity, but neat. Some teams may wear uniforms or closely coordinated outfits.

Therapy. Some therapy organizations have a minimum dress code for volunteer visitors, so check their regulations. Dogs are to be clean and neatly groomed. Owners should also present a neat appearance. Casual is okay, but most groups prefer that you wear clothing other than jeans, tee-shirts, sweats, or other leisure wear. Pockets, a bait pouch, or small back pack may prove useful for carrying therapy identification, tissues, or treats for residents to give to your dog.

During a therapy visit, residents may either come to one room to see the dogs, some of whom perform tricks, or handlers may take their dogs room to room, asking first, if each patient would like to pet a dog. Some people like to go for wheelchair rides with the dogs, lie in bed with them near, or just hold them in their laps.

"There is something magical about the whole process," says Carolyn Bonin, whose two retired show Poms are now therapy dogs. "I think Quincy and Anni understand how much those folks need them. Quincy lies upside down for an hour in the lap of some elderly lady he just met, and he doesn't even do that with me. I don't understand it; I just know the folks feel better, I feel better, and the dogs feel better after one of our sessions."

In addition to casual visits to healthcare facilities, therapy may also take on larger tasks through programs like READ—Reading Education Assistance Dogs, crisis response therapy, or animal assisted therapy (AAT). In AAT, owner and dog work with a patient and therapist using a specific plan to achieve a specific goal; results are documented in a medical record. Crisis response involves more intensive training for dealing with victims in post traumatic situations, such as in New York City following 9/11.

Bette Meredith who does therapy with her Poms, Pattie and Chickie, reports, "I had a lady say the first word she had ever said since coming to the nursing home. She petted Pattie and said, 'Beautiful.' The nurse was thrilled." If you think you and your Pom have what it takes to work a little magic and bring a smile and some cheer to a lonely person, get active with therapy visits.

FUN AND EXERCISE

Not all activity with your Pom has to be structured or competitive. Some of the most fun you have may be playtime around the house or outdoor recreation.

Time spent playing with your Pom is some of the best quality time you can spend together.

Playtime Games

As long as you are paying attention to and playing with him, your Pom will enjoy most types of doggy activity in which the two of you engage. Poms can enjoy squeaky toys, catching Pom-sized balls, and playing tag or peek-a-boo. Hide and seek is an excellent way to teach the "come" command. While your dog isn't looking, you hide, then softly call him to come. When he finds you, give him a treat and praise.

Most dogs enjoy searching for hidden treats. Any game that utilizes the sense of smell is usually fun for a dog. For non-dominant dogs, a careful game of tug is also pleasurable entertainment. Just be careful not to injure tiny teeth, that may already be prone to dental problems.

Tricks

Because they like to be the center of attention and the star of show, some Poms love learning and performing tricks. Using basic obedience commands as the starting point, you can teach your Pom to roll over, shake hands, and play dead. If he has a natural inclination to stand on his (healthy) hind legs, you can also teach him to dance. Other tricks owners can teach a Pom are to put away toys, play basketball on a miniature set, sneeze, whisper (bark softly), and say prayers (sit up on hind legs with front paws together and head down).

If you want to teach your Pom but are uncertain how, there are books available with step-by-step directions for teaching a variety of tricks. Also check the internet. Bulletin boards and e-mail lists for Pom people are a good place to swap "how-to" tips. Combined with therapy visits, a performing Pom can put a smile on many faces.

Poms love to be taken out so they can explore and be admired at the same time.

Walking and Hiking

There's hardly a dog who doesn't love a good walk, and the Pom is no exception. Get out his leash, put on your walking shoes, and your Pom most likely will be waiting eagerly at the door. Since Poms are so small, it doesn't take long for a walk to turn into an endurance event. Plan on starting out with short distances and work up to longer walks. Maximum distance for a small dog is usually 2 miles (3.2 km), but some owners may be able to walk their Poms a little longer.

Most Pomeranians enjoy the outdoors, but if 2 miles (3.2 km) is a long walk, how can you take your Pom on a lengthier excursion? Try using a backpack style carrier or puppy pouch which allows your dog to rest without stopping or tiring you out by carrying him. With a carrier along, your dog can hike for a little while, get carried in the pack a bit, then walk some more when he's ready.

Be cautious about the thick coat and small feet picking up burrs, briars, and thorns, and little legs getting caught or twisted by tree roots and crevices between rocks. Carefully restrain your Pom near the edge of any drop offs. Along with a carrier, take a hydration pack. Include enough water for both of you, a collapsible bowl for him and a small snack or dry meal for day hikes. Keep a brush or comb handy for removing debris collected in the fur.

On a hike or a walk, don't let your dog get too tired, but have fun getting some exercise together; it's healthy for both of you.

Out and About

Poms love to be admired and, like most dogs, they also like to go for car rides. Put the two together and you have the combination for fun on the go with your dog. Poms are great dogs for accompanying you on errands that require a trip to a drive-through. Put your dog in his car seat or portable crate to take him to the bank, drug store, or fast-food restaurant. He'll love the attention and treats he gets from clerks and tellers.

If you enjoy shopping, it may be possible take your Pom with you to your local hardware superstore. Check first, but most allow well behaved dogs on leash in their facilities. Poms easily fit in the carts and win the attention and smiles of other shoppers. Don't forget that friendly dogs on leash are normally welcome to shop at pet supply stores, also.

If you know other Pomeranian owners in your area, why not arrange to get together? While the humans chat and share dog stories and tips, well-behaved and socialized Poms can enjoy a play date. Just make sure your Pom is one who likes the company of strange dogs before putting him with new friends.

Any type of outing, like a trip to an outdoor ice cream stand or a romp in the park, is enjoyable for you and your dog, and an excellent way to teach him how to behave in public, socialize him, and have fun at the same time.

Just Being a Dog

Since Pomeranians are born and bred to be companions, some of the best times you can enjoy are when you and he do nothing but simply spend time together. Combine television time with cuddle time that will make you both happy. Even grooming, a necessity with a Pom, can be a special time for bonding because the two of you are spending time that is focused solely on each other. Whatever task or activity you undertake together, enjoy the pleasure of each other's company. That's part of what loving a dog is all about.

8

HEALTH
of Your Pomeranian

There are several components that come together to make a healthy dog—genetics, nutrition, environment, and exercise—but implementing and maintaining a preventive healthcare program for your Pomeranian, along with watching for symptoms and seeking veterinary treatment as soon as your dog becomes ill, is the basic foundation for giving him a life of wellness.

FIRST AND FUTURE EXAMS

Within 24 to 72 hours of bringing home your new Pomeranian, it is important to schedule a new puppy veterinary examination. This appointment may also be a good opportunity for your dog to meet his veterinarian under less stressful circumstances than when he will be seen in the future for medical treatment.

Your puppy's history will be reviewed and recorded. Any vaccinations that are due will be given. The vet will perform a thorough physical examination and check for internal and external parasites. She will also check your puppy for obvious congenital defects during this first visit. This appointment is a good time to ask any questions about puppy care or behavior. Your vet can provide general information about the common health problems which Pomeranians may develop. You may also wish to discuss a future time to have your dog spayed or neutered.

New Puppy Exam

On his first visit to the vet, your puppy will be weighed and have his:

- Coat condition and skin observed, checked for fleas;
- Stool sample tested for worms;
- Chest, heart and lungs listened to with stethoscope;
- Eyes, ears, mouth, teeth and gums, tongue, throat examined;
- Abdomen palpated;
- Eating and elimination habits described;
- Joints moved and flexed;
- Activity level described.

A lifetime of good health starts with a well-puppy exam, and your Pom should have an annual veterinary check-up every year after. This examination will be similar to the new puppy exam. Blood and urine samples may be taken, and possibly an x-ray. If vaccinations are due, the annual check up is a convenient time to have them given.

Annual well-dog exams are an excellent tool for diagnosing conditions that may just be in the early stages. Additionally, any health problems which your dog might have developed will be monitored at the annual exam. Diets, medications, and treatment plans will be adjusted if necessary. As your Pom ages, special emphasis on preventive health care can give him a more comfortable, longer life with you.

One of the most important responsibilities an owner assumes for his dog is to provide regular, quality veterinary care. There are many elements that make for a healthy dog—genetics, diet, exercise, and environment—but following a strong preventive healthcare program, along with keeping a watchful eye for symptoms of disease and seeking treatment for your Pom, are all key steps to giving him a life of wellness.

THE PERFECT VET FOR YOUR POM

Before you can take your new Pom for his first exam, you need to carefully select a veterinarian, one who is knowledgeable,

Spaying and Neutering

Neutering or spaying is surgical sterilization and results in the loss of ability to produce puppies. Sterilization prevents unplanned litters, as well as many types of cancer and other diseases of the reproductive organs.

Most importantly, neutering reduces the pet population. Although the Pomeranian is a much loved and admired breed, there are still far too many of them who end up unwanted, neglected, and for lack of sufficient available good homes, may be euthanized.

Additionally, the greatest majority of Poms do not have enough outstanding traits to pass on their genes to future generations of the breed and should not be bred. However, if you have hopes of being a real breeder, do your homework!! It take years of study, research, showing, and planning, and is very expensive to produce even one litter of healthy, quality Pomeranian puppies.

Remember—the only reason to have puppies is for betterment of the breed, not for profit, so make an appointment and sterilize your Pom.

compassionate, and with whom you feel comfortable. First, look close to home for quicker transportation time to the clinic, particularly in an emergency. But don't be unwilling to drive a greater distance if the best veterinarian is farther away.

Word of mouth is an excellent way to find a veterinarian. Ask people like your groomer or training instructor—people who talk with many dog owners on a regular basis—which vets they have heard are skilled caregivers. Where do your friends take their dogs? What do they like about the veterinarian, the staff, and the clinic? Referrals may be also obtained through veterinary professional organizations such as the American Veterinary Medical Association (AMVA) or the American Animal Hospital Association (AAHA) at www.healthypet.com.

After narrowing your search, schedule an appointment to meet the new veterinarian and visit her clinic. Find out if the vet has experience with toy dogs, particularly Pomeranians. Is she educated about breed-specific conditions? Is the clinic clean and the staff helpful? Are the hours convenient and the fees reasonable for the services provided? Is the veterinarian willing to speak with you and are you able to understand what she is telling you? Do you feel like you can build a client-patient-doctor relationship that will work?

Don't wait until there is an emergency to choose your veterinarian. Finding a vet in whom you are confident enough to entrust your dog's care is not an easy task. There are many questions you should ask and factors to analyze when making your decision, but personal intuition is important as well. If you don't feel comfortable with a veterinarian, keep looking—your dog's life may depend on your decision.

VACCINATIONS

Protection through vaccination against fatal or life-threatening, infectious diseases is one of the most important aspects of veterinary care. Originally given every year as part of the annual examination, vaccination protocols are currently being redefined by veterinary colleges, professional organizations, as well as manufacturers of vaccines. The possible association of disabling,

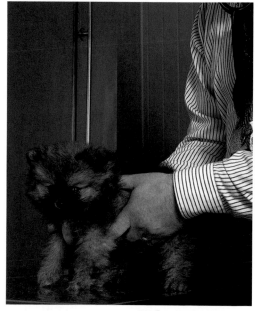

Find a veterinarian with whom you are comfortable so you can feel confident your puppy will be in good hands for a lifetime.

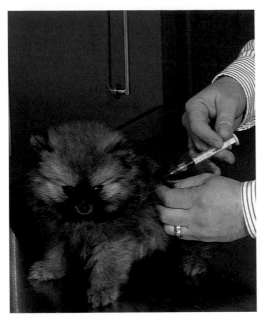

All dogs need protection from certain potentially fatal diseases. Discuss with your veterinarian a vaccine protocol for your puppy.

chronic illness due to what may be excessive vaccination has been the main reason given for this change.

Even with changing schedules, it is still important for your dog to be vaccinated. Decide with your veterinarian how often you will vaccinate and for which diseases. Vaccines (immunization against viruses) for the most prevalent and potentially lethal diseases come in either individual products or in combination for multiple viruses.

Illnesses

Your Pom may be vaccinated against the following illnesses:

Rabies

This fatal virus attacks the nervous system and causes encephalitis. Rabies is transmitted in saliva from animals such as raccoons, foxes, skunks, bats, and infected domestic animals who bite. Symptoms include personality changes, fever, aggression, salivation, paralysis, and death. Vaccination is done at between the ages of three months and one year, then every three years. Rabies vaccines are mandatory by law, and in a few states are required every year. Your veterinarian will be able to inform you of the requirements in your state.

Distemper

Extremely contagious, this virus affects the lining of many organs including the eyes, respiratory system, gastrointestinal system, and brain. Symptoms include fever, loss of appetite, dehydration, mucous discharge, hard calluses on the foot pads, vomiting, and diarrhea. Infection leads to death in nearly all cases, with very few dogs making a full recovery from the disease. Puppies are vaccinated at ages 8, 12, and 16 weeks.

Parvovirus

Another highly contagious virus, parvo is transmitted through feces. The virus is difficult to kill and can be carried on clothing, feet, and fur, as well as live in contaminated crates, bedding, and bowls. Loss of appetite, profuse and sometimes bloody vomiting and diarrhea, and a high fever are the main symptoms. Puppies contract the disease most frequently and become severely ill or die, often within a few hours. Vaccination schedules for parvo vary, but usually start at 6 to 8 weeks of age and are given every three to four weeks, with a possible additional booster at age 16 or 20 weeks.

Hepatitis

A virus that attacks the liver, kidneys, and lining of the blood vessels, hepatitis is transmitted through urine, feces, and saliva. The disease takes multiple forms, ranging from mild to fatal, with symptoms that include high fever, loss of appetite, bloody vomit and diarrhea, abdominal pain, and jaundice. Immunizations are given at ages 8 and 12 weeks.

Kennel Cough Complex

KCC is a group of highly contagious diseases that cause bronchitis and inflammation of the throat, resulting in a deep, spasmodic, hacking cough. The most common causes of KCC are the **parainfluenza** virus or the **bordetella** bacteria, and the illness is sometimes known by these names. Both are easily spread through droplets sprayed during sneezing or coughing, and via contaminated bowls, bedding, and so forth. Both types of KCC are largely preventable through immunization.

Parainfluenza vaccine can be administered in conjunction with distemper or hepatitis shots, or by intranasal spray as early as 2 weeks of age. The bordetella bacterin (immunization against a bacterial infection) is also available for intranasal administration, or as an injection. Annual immunization against bordetella is recommended for any dog who is frequently around other dogs, such as in a kennel or at dog shows.

Dogs that are frequently exposed to other dogs should receive the bordetella vaccine.

Leptospirosis

This bacterial infection is transmitted in the soil, from wildlife, and through the urine of infected dogs. Lepto is more prevalent in some regions of the country than others. There are multiple strains of leptospirosis but the main symptoms are fever, inappetence, nausea and vomiting, and pain. Complications are common and include kidney failure, liver damage, dehydration, internal bleeding, hemorrhage, and death. Immunization can be done at ages 9, 12, and 15 weeks.

Coronavirus

Coronavirus is a virus that affects the gastrointestinal system and causes foul-smelling, bright yellow or orange diarrhea. Other symptoms may include loss of appetite, depression, and vomiting. Most cases are mild and self-limiting, but puppies and debilitated dogs can become quite ill or even die. Vaccination against corona is recommended for dogs who are in frequent contact with other dogs. The suggested schedule of vaccination is two doses 2 to 3 weeks apart. It is also available in a multi-component vaccine.

Lyme Disease

If your dog is bitten by a deer tick, he is at risk for Lyme disease. Symptoms of this chronic bacterial infection include depressed appetite, weight loss, lethargy, fever, and primarily lameness and swollen joints. Possible development of arthritis and heart inflammation can occur. Immunization is available against Lyme, but the bacterin's effectiveness is still being studied and is recommended only for dogs that live in areas with high tick infestation or who spend a great deal of time in the woods.

If you suspect an adverse reaction to a vaccination, contact your vet immediately for follow-up.

Vaccination Protocol

Based on a slowly growing body of evidence, many veterinarians are recommending that booster immunizations be given every three years instead of every year. Additionally, the criteria for determining which vaccines to administer are being evaluated. Vaccines have been divided into two groups: core and non-core vaccinations. Core vaccines are for diseases that are life-threatening or fatal if contracted. Non-core vaccinations are advised for dogs who have a greater than average risk of being exposed to the infectious agent, partially based on whether or not the region where they live has a high occurrence of the disease.

Based on your Pom's current health status and his medical

history, how often he is in contact with multiple other dogs, the type of activities in which you and he engage, and his risk of having an adverse or chronic reaction as the result of vaccination, your veterinarian will recommend which vaccines your dog should receive and how often.

COMMON HEALTH PROBLEMS IN THE POMERANIAN

Although the Pomeranian, as a Nordic dog, is by nature hardy and healthy, that doesn't meant that the breed is exempt from health problems. A few conditions are more likely to occur in Toy dogs simply because of their size, while others have a genetic component and may occur slightly more often in the Pomeranian than most other breeds.

While most responsible breeders plan their litters to avoid inheritable conditions and to maximize the potential for good health in their dogs, because the Pomeranian is such a popular companion animal, there are individuals who sell puppies only for profit, breeding any available dog regardless of his health status.

"If you are buying a puppy, you should be able to look at the parents. Check out the health condition of the parents. Be aware of what you are purchasing," recommends Florida veterinarian and Pomeranian owner Kandra L. Jones, DVM. "Have the puppy checked out by a veterinarian within three days of purchasing him. If the vet feels there are problems, then discuss them with the breeder."

The best way to avoid many health problems in a new puppy

Vaccination Reactions

Immediate or Short-Term: It is possible for your dog to be feverish and lethargic, lose his appetite, and experience swelling or discomfort at the injection site for 24 to 48 hours after he has been vaccinated. These symptoms are mild, and normally pose no health threat. But vaccinations can result in more serious, allergic reactions which can be fatal.

Symptoms of an allergic response are itching, hives, swelling of the face and head, vomiting or diarrhea. Allergic reactions can progress into anaphylactic shock. Symptoms are the same as an allergic reaction but are worse and also include swelling of the eyelids, tongue and throat, fluid in the lungs, wheezing, difficulty breathing, restlessness, rapid heartbeat, collapse, convulsions, coma, and death.

Small dogs like the Pom may be more prone to allergic reactions because of their size. If your dog shows any of these symptoms within a few minutes or hours after receiving a vaccine, seek veterinary treatment immediately.

Delayed or Long-Term: The most common side effect from vaccination is believed to be possible over-stimulation of the immune system, which may result in autoimmune disease, a condition in which the body attacks and gradually destroys its own tissues or organs. Vaccination-related autoimmune diseases can affect the joints, kidneys, blood or vascular system, the skin, nervous system, or gastrointestinal tract. Symptoms are widely varied.

Besides a misdirected immune system, the opposite is possible and resistance to other infectious diseases may be reduced. Some veterinarians believe that recurring ear and bladder infections might be one sign of this condition.

The long-term effects of frequent, repeated vaccination are just beginning to be studied. If you have concerns about the possible effect of vaccinations on your dog's health, discuss them with your veterinarian.

is by finding an ethical, reputable breeder who genetically tests her dogs and breeds only the healthiest Poms, whose relatives were also healthy.

Luxating Patellas

Patellar luxation, the technical term for a slipped kneecap, is the top orthopedic problem in the Pomeranian. Although the condition can occur as a result of trauma, the majority of cases of this congenital disorder are hereditary.

A luxating patella occurs because the femur (long thigh bone) develops abnormally, which in turn pulls on the thigh muscle attached to the patella (kneecap). As a result, the bones and ligaments of the knee are misaligned and become deformed due to constant orthopedic stress. It is also possible that the groove in the thigh bone, which aligns and holds the kneecap in place, is not deep enough to prevent improper movement out of the joint. This condition usually manifests midway between puppyhood and adulthood, or in young adult dogs.

Instead of walking normally, a dog with a luxating patella may take a "skipping" step, and will experience intermittent periods of lameness and discomfort. Another possible sign of patellar luxation is if he stops walking and stretches his leg out behind him in an attempt to get the kneecap to slip back into place. Or the dog may walk in a crouched position as the condition worsens. Additionally, arthritis is likely to develop in the affected joint.

Patellar luxation appears in varying degrees of severity. The least problematic is a subluxated patella, which results in a mild tendency towards joint weakness and limited episodes of temporary misalignment. In most cases the kneecap returns to its proper position on its own. Treatment is normally not necessary for subluxation because there seldom is long term damage to the joint.

However, the remaining degrees of luxation—rated as a grade 2, 3, or 4—indicate a progressive state which typically worsens over the years with normal usage of the leg. The higher the grade number, the more severe the degree of luxation. Surgery is the treatment of choice to repair and realign the joint. Keep in mind that some Pom breeders feel it is best to wait until the dog is about 18 months old before any corrective surgery is performed, as some dogs may outgrow a minor problem. Your veterinarian can give you some guidance as to whether waiting is appropriate or not for your pet. If your Pom shows signs of patellar luxation, seek veterinary attention to reduce the level of his pain and the likelihood of future deterioration of the joint

Pomeranians who are prone to patellar luxation should not be permitted to jump off of raised surfaces such as a grooming table. Ramps may prove helpful for getting on and off of beds or furniture without jumping, which could help slow the progression of joint and leg damage. Care should also be taken to avoid certain types of exercise and prevent obesity, both of which can further strain an affected joint.

Hypoglycemia

Hypoglycemia is the medical term for low blood sugar. Glucose, the form of "sugar" that circulates in the body, is the final product obtained when foods, particularly carbohydrates as found in fruits, vegetables, grains, sugars, are metabolized. It is the body's primary and most readily-available source of energy. Levels of glucose are regulated by insulin, a hormone released by the pancreas. Excess glucose is stored first in the liver as glycogen, then around the body as fat. Because tiny toy dogs such as the Pom cannot always maintain sufficient stores of glycogen, they may be prone to episodes of hypoglycemia.

Episodic hypoglycemia tends most frequently to affect puppies approximately ages 6 to 16 weeks. Poms are high-energy, active dogs who burn a lot of calories—and glucose—during play. Because of their small size, their bodies cannot store and generate enough blood sugar for their activity level, particularly as young, growing pups.

Signs that your Pom's blood glucose may be dropping too low include sluggishness, weakness, confusion or unusual behavior, depression, drowsiness, staggering, chills, pale gums, shaking and tremors, dilated pupils, convulsions, collapse, or possibly coma. Not every puppy will experience all these symptoms, so watch your pup closely for a sudden onset of any of these signs.

A puppy that is observed to be experiencing an episode of hypoglycemia should receive treatment immediately. Many breeders

Poms are prone to patellar luxation, or slipped kneecaps, which manifest as walking with a funny step or in a crouched position, usually when the dog is a young adult.

If your puppy suddenly appears confused, weak, or chilled, he may be experiencing low blood sugar.

recommend keeping a supply of Nutrical—a flavored product packed with sugars and vitamins—on hand. Karo syrup can also be used in an emergency. Rub the sugar substance on the gums until your dog begins licking. Afterwards try to get the dog to eat a nutrient-dense meal.

If the dog has lost consciousness, this is a serious emergency. Seek veterinary treatment. Intravenous fluids with dextrose may be necessary to treat swelling of the brain caused by the drop in blood sugar levels. Hypoglycemia is not a trivial problem. Repeated occurrences can cause permanent brain damage.

Although most puppies outgrow this condition, it is possible for some adult Pomeranians to be hypoglycemic throughout their lives. Attacks can be precipitated by missing a meal, illness, getting chilled or overly tired, nervousness, or new situations that induce high levels of anxiety. To prevent the problem, try free-choice feeding of a premium, calorie-dense kibble, oversee playtime so that your Pom doesn't exceed his limits, and keep him warm during cold weather.

Dental Problems

Retained Deciduous (Baby) Teeth

Puppies are usually born with 28 baby teeth that begin to emerge around 3 or 4 weeks of age. In small breeds like the Pom, these teeth come in more slowly than in larger dogs, and by age 6 to 9 weeks, all types of the deciduous teeth should be present.

Somewhere between the ages of 4 or 5 months, and lasting for about 2 to 3 months, the adult, or permanent teeth begin to erupt. Normally, the roots of the baby teeth are being reabsorbed during this time as the permanent teeth push the deciduous teeth completely out. Puppies tend to chew more during this period, which helps the process along. However, in Toy dogs such as the Pomeranian, it is not uncommon for the baby teeth to be retained (remain in place) as the adult teeth grow in. The problem may first be noticed when a dog opens his mouth and it appears as if there is a double set of teeth, or a small tooth is overlapping a larger one.

Retained baby teeth can cause the development of a malocclusion (bad bite) that lasts a lifetime. Not only do malocclusions look funny, they are a source of pain when chewing and can contribute to dental decay. Because Poms can easily retain baby teeth, it is strongly advised that the bite be checked frequently from about 3 months of age on through the entire teething period, to catch any problems that might be developing. Treatment of retained deciduous teeth is removal by a veterinarian.

Tooth Loss

"Dog or human, the most common cause of tooth loss in any species is periodontal disease," says Paty Aird, Certified Dental Assistant and Pomeranian owner. Periodontal disease is also the main cause of oral infection and manifests in two ways—gingivitis and periodontitis.

Normal, healthy gum tissue is pink, but in gingivitis the gums turn bright red due to inflammation. A dog with gingivitis may also have bad breath, experience discomfort when chewing, and his gums may bleed. **Gingivitis** is primarily caused by the build-up of plaque (soft, whitish, sticky material composed of decaying food and bacteria) around the gum-line.

As gingivitis progresses, the gums may recede from the teeth and small pockets develop. These pockets trap more food and bacteria, generate more plaque and more gingivitis in a self-perpetuating cycle. Eventually, pus may form, causing the dog more discomfort along with a possible decrease in appetite. Untreated gingivitis frequently leads to periodontitis.

As plaque builds up on teeth, and gums become more and more inflamed, it hardens into tartar, also known as calculus because it contains calcium-based substances. Unlike plaque, tartar is yellowish to brown and has rough edges which also build up around the gum-line. While plaque in the early stages can be removed by basic brushing, calculus cannot. Some smaller breeds have a greater tendency to deposit more plaque and tartar on their teeth than other breeds.

Periodontitis ensues when the structures that hold teeth in place are gradually destroyed by the ever-increasing amounts of bacteria. Teeth are held onto the bone by connective tissue known as the periodontal membrane or ligament. It is this tissue, along with the bone and the roots of the teeth destroyed by infection, eventually causing teeth to loosen and fall out.

"Since Poms have such tiny teeth, the roots and ligaments are very

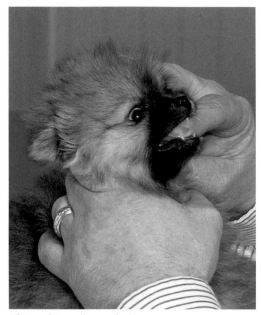

The condition of your dog's teeth and gums is something that should be monitored throughout your Pom's lifetime.

small, so it doesn't take as much bone loss, or as long for the gums to recede and cause the teeth to come out," Aird explains. "It's not that calculus builds up faster for Poms; they just have such tiny teeth that it doesn't take long to compromise the integrity of their teeth."

The best method for treating periodontal disease is to prevent it by feeding dry kibble, regularly brushing your Pom's teeth, and providing him with safe chew toys that also help keep teeth clean. However, if your Pom already has either gingivitis or periodontitis, these conditions need treatment by a veterinarian. Treatment methods include scaling and removal of plaque or tartar, normally under sedation or general anesthesia, possible trimming of gingival tissue that can't be saved, or removal of affected teeth and repair of the bone structure.

If periodontal disease is not too advanced, it is possible, in some cases, that the teeth can be saved and reattach themselves. Antibiotics are normally given to prevent the spread of infection and the veterinarian may advise cleaning your dog's teeth with a special, hydrogen peroxide-based solution at home.

Collapsing Trachea

The trachea (windpipe) is the tube that serves as the passage for air moving between the mouth and lungs. It is supported in its normal, open position by bands (rings) of cartilage. In Toy dogs, these rings can weaken and collapse, which in turn reduces the flow of air and causes coughing.

At one time, collapsing tracheas were thought to be an acquired condition, but current veterinary texts note that metabolic deficiencies have been found in some dogs that cause tracheal cartilage to develop less rigidly than is necessary for proper support. Tracheal collapse can be caused by trauma, but this occurs less frequently, or may just be the incident which triggers symptoms of the preexisting condition.

Signs of a collapsing trachea may begin gradually, usually sometime in early- to mid-adulthood and older. These signs may have been present for some time, but have not been detected due to the intermittent nature of the early stages of the collapse. Typically, symptoms include a honking cough, and episodic coughing, along with possible shallow breathing, gagging, or coughing-up of mucous which is often mistaken for vomiting. Fainting may occur if the coughing lasts long enough and air intake is sufficiently restricted.

Collapse can either be partial or total, and can occur in two different regions of the trachea: upper, more in the throat (cervical); or lower, more towards the lungs (intrathoracic). Cervical collapse tends to occur when the dog inhales. During this type of collapse it is also possible for part of the tracheal membrane to drop down into the airway, causing additional irritation and coughing. Collapse of the lower trachea happens during exhalation of the breath. Other, small airways may also be weakened and close at the same time, increasing cough and inflammation.

Tracheal collapse is found more frequently in poorly bred Poms, such as those from puppy mills, or Poms which are overweight. Although many dogs will be normal between episodes, stress, hot weather or overly warm indoor temperatures, high humidity, and excitement can all actuate the problem. Other triggers include exercise, eating, drinking, inhaling smoke or other irritants, pressure on the throat (such as from a leash pulling a collar too tightly) and respiratory infections.

If your Pom has episodes of a honking cough while gasping for air, have him checked for tracheal collapse. The vet will listen thoroughly to your dog's throat and chest while he breathes, palpate his throat area and probably take x-rays. If the problem is more severe, the vet may also perform a tracheal wash or a bronchoscopy to look for additional issues that could complicate the condition.

Treatment is usually aimed at controlling the factors which trigger a collapse and at reducing symptoms during an episode. Weight loss is recommended for Poms who are obese although exercise must be reduced in frequency and intensity. Efforts must be made to control exposure to hot and humid environments, as well as to irritants such as smoke, or even fragrances which can incite an episode of coughing.

Oral Health

An important note about dental disease: the bacteria found in plaque and calculus can spread to other organs such as the heart or kidneys, and cause serious, possibly life-threatening disease. So even when it's inconvenient or difficult, make the effort to brush your Pom's teeth on a regular basis. In the meantime, watch for signs that your Pom may be developing dental problems. For most conditions, signs include pawing at the mouth, difficulty chewing, loss of appetite or disinterest in food and chew toys, drooling or excessive salivation, bad breath, bleeding or red gums, discomfort or pain when chewing. If some of these symptoms are present, consult your veterinarian.

Medications that may be used include cough suppressants, a limited course of anti-inflammatories to reduce irritation, or possibly bronchodilators, which increase the lungs' ability to handle air. If a secondary infection is present, antibiotics may also be prescribed.

Surgery is not recommended if lifestyle changes and medication can control the symptoms. However in some dogs, particularly those with more frequent or total collapse, surgery to support the trachea with prosthetic (artificial) rings may be recommended. This surgery is described as a high-risk procedure and should only be performed by a specialist skilled in the technique.

Although tracheal collapse is an irreversible condition, it is possible to control the symptoms reasonably well. The good news is that the condition is seldom life-threatening. And, even though a Pom with a collapsing trachea may need to be less active, a happy, normal life is still possible.

Severe Hair Loss Syndrome

Hair loss—alopecia, in technical terms—does not refer to normal shedding, but more extensive loss of fur over large areas of the body that become bald as a result. There are many causes of alopecia, the most common being flea and other allergies, mange, stress, Cushing's Disease, and hypothyroidism (low thyroid levels). However, Pomeranians are also prone to a type of hair loss that is usually unrelated to these causes.

Because the exact mechanisms that cause the hair loss and related skin problems have not precisely been determined, the name of the condition also varies. It may be referred to as alopecia X, black skin disease, pseudo-Cushing's disease, elephant skin disease, one of multiple sex-hormone associated dermatoses or growth hormone (GH)-responsive alopecia, also known as hyposomatotropism. Due to all the confusion in names and causes, the American Pomeranian Club proposed referring to the condition in Pomeranians as "severe hair loss syndrome" (SHLS).

The syndrome tends to appear at puberty or in young adults, although dogs of any age can acquire the condition. Both sides of the body lose hair in symmetric patches, usually striking the trunk, back of the thighs, neck, tail, and ears. Hair loss may be total or just affect the guard hairs, sparing the undercoat. The fur that does remain often becomes dry and coarse, and breaks or falls out easily. Coat color may also change, acquiring a reddish tint.

Before the fur falls out, the disease may remain undetected, only to be found if the Pom is clipped during grooming and the hair fails to regrow. Additionally, seasonal shedding may fail to occur. Once the fur is lost, hyperpigmentation (darkening of the skin) usually develops, and may be so intense that the skin appears black. The skin may also thicken or become thinner.

If your dog is experiencing unusual hair loss, speak to your veterinarian about it.

Testing

Prior to beginning any treatment, careful testing should be done to rule out other conditions such as thyroid disease. A thorough history and physical exam comes first. Skin scrapings or a biopsy may be needed. X-rays may be taken to detect the presence of tumors which might have caused the imbalance and resultant hair loss. Blood and urine are collected and analyzed.

In dogs with GH-responsive alopecia, most of these basic test results are normal, including thyroid and adrenal function. At this point, sex hormone levels may be tested and estrogen, progesterone, or testosterone may be discovered to be either too high or too low. It is possible to measure growth hormone levels but the expensive test is not without risk and is not readily available to most primary care veterinarians.

"Treatment and diagnosis begins with the primary veterinarian," Dr. Jones says. "Some vets may choose to refer cases of this nature if they don't feel comfortable [dealing] with endocrine disorders. But usually, any vet should be capable of diagnosing and treating these [hair loss] disorders."

Treatment

Once other conditions have been ruled out, treatment options can be considered. First, if the dog has not been spayed or neutered, this should be done, as it corrects SHLS in many cases in fertile dogs.

But be aware that the disease may return—the condition is seen just as frequently in dogs who have already been sterilized. Depending on the levels of various hormones, sex hormones specific to the deficiency or imbalance may be administered. Side effects can be serious and include anemia, bone marrow suppression, aggressive behavior, or liver damage.

Growth hormone levels may be supplemented if other therapy is not appropriate. GH is given by injection over several days and in multiple treatments. Synthesized GH may be expensive and difficult to obtain. After about a month or slightly longer, hair may begin to regrow. Symptoms can return in as little as six months, but remission from the disease may last for a few years following treatment.

Yeast

Another possible cause of SHLS and black skin may be related to a fungal growth, Malassezia yeast. This yeast has been found in chronic ear inflammations, irritation of skin that rubs together such as the arm pit and chest, and in general dermatitis related to oily, scaly skin. Like other causes, early signs such as slight redness, mild itchiness, presence of yellowish dander, or excess oil may be missed, and the condition undetected until the hair is lost. Noticeable symptoms are the same—extensive hair loss and darkening of the skin.

Before attempting to treat for a yeast infection, a thorough veterinary exam and testing is warranted to rule out other causes. In most cases, a correct culture for the presence of Malassezia overgrowth should be found to make the diagnosis. Veterinary treatment usually consists of administration of an oral anti-fungal drug, bathing in special shampoo, and possibly a combination anti-bacterial/anti-fungal dip. Dogs undergoing treatment should be monitored about every two weeks until the condition clears and treatment is completed.

The Health and Genetics Committee of the American Pomeranian Club has a suggested guideline for treatment at home, based on a British veterinary study. Begin by rubbing the dog with a degreasing hand cleaner, then rinse with water or wash off with mild, diluted anti-bacterial dish detergent. Bathe in an anti-fungal shampoo which contains chlorhexiderm and allow it to remain on the coat and skin for 15 minutes, then rinse. If a water-only rinse was used following application of hand cleaner, now bathe with the dish detergent as described above. Dry the dog thoroughly to eliminate damp spots that may promote fungal growth. Repeat every three days for three weeks. Wash and disinfect grooming tools between every use (on each dog, if multiple dogs are in the household).

If Malassezia yeast is a contributing factor to SHLS, after cleansing as above, hair regrowth may be seen in just a few weeks. Yeast overgrowth can occur concurrent with other health problems, so return to the vet clinic if symptoms recur; multiple causes and conditions may need to be addressed.

While SHLS causes a drastic change in a Pom's appearance, in most instances it is not a serious condition and affected dogs can lead normal lives. Just remember to keep a hair-challenged dog warm, and dress him in sweaters during chilly weather.

If your Pom has extensive hair loss and darkening of the skin, schedule an appointment for a complete veterinary consultation. Your vet will be able to help determine what the cause of your dog's alopecia might be and suggest a treatment plan with which you and your dog can live, and hopefully regrow hair.

Other Problems

Other potential health problems to be aware of, if you are getting a Pomeranian, include chronic bronchitis, epilepsy, hypothyroidism, age-related heart disease, tiny legs which break easily, and risk of side effects from general anesthesia.

Anesthesia Reactions

Because of their size, Poms can react badly or even die while under anesthesia. If your Pom needs anesthesia, be mindful that the risk may be reduced if procedures are

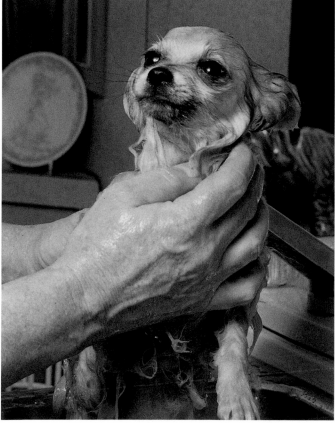

Bathing with a specially formulated shampoo is part of the protocol for relieving skin and coat conditions.

short, or if only one procedure is done at a time. "Anesthesia is never without risk," explains Dr. Jones, "The anesthetic I prefer to use on a

Pom is propofol intravenously, then sevoflurane gas for maintenance." Ask your vet questions about the procedure and type of anesthesia if you are concerned.

Inheriting SHLS

Pomeranians who have SHLS, or whose relatives suffer from the condition, should not be bred. Although it has not been proven that the disease is passed genetically, certain breeds — including the Pomeranian — are clearly predisposed to the problem, which indicates that a tendency to inherit SHLS may exist.

Broken Legs

The best bets for broken legs are caution and prevention. Keep your Pom from jumping from high furniture. If he jumps onto a surface which is too high for a safe dismount, lift him down. A ramp may be useful if your Pom insists on getting up on elevated furnishings, such as a high bed, to sleep with you. And always set him down off the grooming table. Also watch out for stepping on little paws and legs with a Pom who likes to walk close to your feet.

Chronic Bronchitis

Chronic bronchitis causes intermittent episodes of coughing, but instead of being trachea-related, the condition is related to inflammation of the lungs. Symptoms may occur more often in overweight dogs, or those who are repeatedly exposed to irritants in the air.

Epilepsy

Epilepsy is a neurological disorder that affects how electrical impulses are conducted in certain parts of the brain. Dogs with epilepsy have repeated episodes of seizures that can either be mild or severe. If your Pom has a seizure, take him to the vet immediately. Epileptic seizures can cause brain damage. Medications may need to be administered for the remainder of the dog's life, and dosages or types may need readjusted periodically. Affected Poms should be prevented from becoming anxious or overly stressed.

Hypothyroidism

Hypothyroidism is a condition in which the thyroid gland does not produce enough thyroid hormone. Many bodily functions and organ systems can be negatively impacted, including the heart. Hypothyroidism may stand alone as a problem or be part of another disease process. If your dog gains weight easily, has thinning fur, is lethargic, and maybe has bulging eyes or a nasty change in personality, ask your vet about a possible thyroid problem. Once a diagnosis has been made, treatment is usually simple—a daily dose of thyroid hormone. Thyroid levels will need to be monitored as long as your dog is on meds, and regular trips to the vet to watch for the development of other related conditions will be necessary.

Heart Disease

Age-related heart diseases can happen to any breed, not just a Pom. There are many different conditions requiring different treatments. A few signs that indicate your senior dog may be acquiring a heart condition are coughing, difficulty breathing, labored breathing after exertion, shortness of breath, or swelling of the legs. Other symptoms may be noticeable, but vary depending on the type of heart problem. If you suspect your Pom has a heart problem, have him checked by a veterinarian. Some cardiac conditions can be managed through medication and lifestyle changes.

Whatever your Pom's health problems may be, if you notice signs that he is not feeling well, schedule an appointment for a veterinary check-up. Prevention and early treatment are often the keys to maintaining a life of good health.

PARASITES

Although owners don't like to think of their cuddly little Poms crawling with fleas or other creepy creatures, it's not uncommon for dogs to become infested with parasites, both internal and external. Parasites are so common, some owners may take their co-existence with their dogs as just a nasty fact of life with a pet. However, parasites can cause serious health problems and should never be ignored.

External Parasites

Fleas

With warm weather or outdoor play, the chance of your dog getting fleas is quite high if he and his environment are unprotected. And, the thick, long coat of the Pom provides the perfect haven in which fleas can hide.

If swallowed, fleas, most commonly, can cause a tapeworm infestation. Long-term flea infestation can result in anemia, which can be serious, even deadly, in puppies or very small dogs.

Some Pomeranians can have an allergic reaction to flea saliva that

You know your dog best and will be able to tell when something seems "off." Monitor your Pom and let the veterinarian know about your concerns.

is injected into a dog's skin when he is bitten. Flea allergy dermatitis, or FAD, causes extreme itching, scratching, and chewing. FAD is treated by bathing the dog and applying a soothing spray. Dietary supplementation with fatty acids also helps. An antihistamine or corticosteroid may be administered by your veterinarian to stop the allergic reaction.

The most important way to treat flea related problems is by keeping your Pom flea free. At the start of flea season, apply a 30-day, topical spoticide if your veterinarian recommends it as safe for your Pom. Spoticides work by killing adult fleas and interrupting the growth cycle (IGRs) of developing fleas. Dogs that are sensitive to spoticides, which cling to the coat for three to four weeks, may need to be dipped by a veterinarian in a special flea-killer instead. Or ask about a preventive spray that can be applied lightly to the coat a few times weekly prior to going outdoors. Monthly oral preventives are also available, but first make sure your veterinarian thinks this is the safest route for your Pom.

If your dog already has fleas, as detected by black flecks in the fur, repeated scratching, and red bumpy bites, you will need to treat him and his environment to get rid of the pests. Bathe him in a flea shampoo recommended by your vet. A water-based spray containing IGRs and made from chrysanthemums and labeled as pyrethrins (natural form) or permethrins (synthetic form), can be applied afterwards. A spoticide may then be used, but you must wait 48 hours after a bath before applying.

Outdoors, areas that promote flea reproduction also need to be treated. Remove dead leaves, grass, pine needles, or other organic debris. Fleas thrive in the shady, moist environments underneath these materials. Apply a pesticide weekly for three weeks by diluting and spraying with water. Permethrin or chlorpyrifos are some chemicals suggested by professionals as either less harmful to pets or as more effective against fleas. Keep your dog out of chemically treated areas for the time recommended by the product's manufacturer.

Inside, wash all dog bedding and vacuum all carpets and upholstered furniture. Sodium polyborate powder can then be applied to carpeted areas. This flea eliminator is purported to have little if any toxicity and be effective for almost a full year. Surfaces may also be sprayed with products containing IGRs, or pyrethrins or permethrins, which are also effective and safer for pets than indoor chemical insecticides containing organophosphates or carbamates. Be cautious when treating your dog, the house, and the yard. Combining multiple chemicals can be a recipe for a sick dog. For the safest recommendations on complete flea removal and control, consult your veterinarian.

Ticks

Dog ticks, deer ticks, and others are blood-sucking parasites that live in brushy woods on common wildlife such as deer, squirrel, and rabbits—or in your yard and on your dog.

Ticks start out tiny, attaching themselves to a dog in hidden places like behind the ears, in the armpits, or on the inside of the legs in order to draw blood and feed. As they become engorged with blood, the ticks grow larger and eventually lay eggs on the host dog. With their tough exterior shell, ticks are difficult to kill.

Ticks should not be viewed as merely a disgusting insect. They are carriers of very serious diseases. If bitten, dogs can become infected with a variety of tickborne illnesses which are difficult to diagnose and treat. These diseases are debilitating, and can induce a critical anemia, result in permanent damage to joints, or bring about a chronic disease state. Many cases can be fatal or cause life-threatening heart, kidney, or liver damage.

Like fleas, prevention is the best approach to managing ticks. Mow areas where your dog plays outside and keep them clear of

Don't let the threat of parasites keep you from getting out with your Pom. Your veterinarian can recommend a flea and tick preventive that will protect him.

fast-growing weeds. If you are using a spoticide or spray-on flea preventive, choose one that incorporates a tick repellant or killer.

Any ticks that your dog does get should be removed immediately. Carefully use a pair of tweezers to pluck the tick—body and head—from your dog's skin, then thoroughly cleanse the bite with alcohol. Follow-up cleaning can be done with a little hydrogen peroxide on a cotton ball.

Symptoms of tickborne disease can show up over a long range of time, from within a week to a few months after a bite. If your Pom shows signs of lameness, weakness, or any other indication that he doesn't feel well after removal of a tick, take him to the veterinarian and request a tick panel.

Mange Mites

There are three types of mange in dogs, all caused by a different type of mite. Each type has a predilection for attacking different areas of the body. Scabies, or sarcoptic mange, usually effects dogs living in dirty conditions and can be passed to humans. Other types are cheyletiellosis, also known as "walking dandruff," and demodectic mange. Puppies contract the latter types more often than adult dogs. Dogs with demodectic mange seem to have a genetic predisposition to damage to the skin. To kill the mites, a veterinarian must prescribe the application of a topical insecticide. Oral medications may also be given to help relieve itching, promote healing, and reduce the chance of recurrence.

Tick-Borne Diseases

Diseases that dogs can acquire from ticks are either caused by a protozoan (a microorganism that can cause disease) or a rickettsia, a type of bacteria. Tick-induced diseases are usually treated with long-term, multiple-antibiotic therapy, plus any other medications as needed to treat additional symptoms, including anti-inflammatories for swollen joints or transfusions for severe anemia.

- **Lyme disease:** Fever, lameness, swollen joints, may affect nervous system, heart, and kidneys. Becomes chronic.

- **Ehrlichiosis:** Loss of appetite, lethargy, stiff achy muscles and joints, upper respiratory symptoms; chronic phase with weakness, swelling, enlarged spleen, bone marrow suppression and anemia, organ failure. High fatality rate.

- **Rocky Mountain spotted fever:** Lethargy, inflammation of the eyes, fever, inappetence, coughing, shortness of breath, vomiting or diarrhea, swelling, staggering gait, seizures; chronic phase with bleeding disorders, hemorrhaging, blood in urine or feces, organ failure; death.

- **Babesiosis:** May not produce symptoms, but can be severe when symptoms are present, including anemia and destruction of red blood cells, enlarged spleen and liver, fever.

Internal Parasites

Thinking about a dog having worms may be enough to make an owner's stomach turn. But it is not uncommon for dogs to have intestinal or other internal parasites at some point in their lives. Many puppies are born with worms, even when the dam appears parasite free or has been wormed prior to conception. Except for heartworms, worms are not a frequent cause of disease in dogs.

However, any infestation should be treated.

Heartworms

These worms are transmitted through the bite of infected mosquitoes. Once infected, the worm's larvae travel through the blood to the right chamber of the heart, where they spend several months maturing. Signs of heartworm infection include coughing, which is sometimes bloody, weakness, shortness of breath, exercise intolerance, and lethargy. Heartworm disease is well advanced by the time symptoms are present. Permanent heart damage or disease is possible, as is death.

To prevent your dog from becoming infested with this life-threatening parasite, place him on preventive. Be cautious when you choose which product to use, as dosing in some brands may be

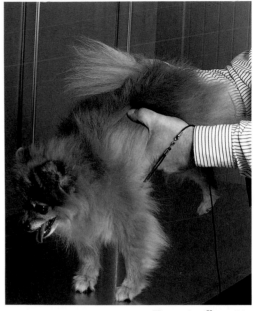

Your vet will want to carefully inspect any areas you think may be infected with mange.

too high, even in the lowest dosage, for a tiny Pomeranian. Even though your dog is on preventive, it is still important to have his blood tested every spring for the presence of heartworm microfilaria (the larval stage). If you are just starting your Pom on heartworm prevention for the first time, also make sure to test for the parasite first as dogs who are given the preventive and are positive for heartworms may go into anaphylactic shock (see first-aid section below) and die.

Should your dog test positive for heartworms, your veterinarian will prescribe medication which must be administered in the clinic, with your dog in observation. Treatment can have serious, even fatal side effects and may take several months before your dog is heartworm clear. So, like most parasites, prevention is the best cure. Plus, an added benefit of giving heartworm preventive is that it also helps prevent most other types of worms.

Tapeworms

To obtain the nutrients on which it feeds, this nematode attaches its head by suckers and hooks to the wall of a dog's intestine. This worm, which can grow to several feet, is composed of reproducing segments. Each segment resembles moist, mobile grains of cooked rice and are passed in your dog's feces. Segments may also crawl around near the anus. After tapeworm sections have been shed, they

Threadworms

This helminth, which is small like the hookworm, is found in soil or passed through feces, and occasionally by the worm's larvae through the skin. If signs are noticeable, they include watery diarrhea and symptoms of lung infection.

look like dried rice grains in the stool.

Tapeworm infestation can cause mild diarrhea, reduced appetite, and possibly weight loss. Fur may become dull as a result of long-term infestation. Besides swallowing fleas which carry tapeworms, dogs can also acquire them from eating wild animals. Prescription medication is necessary to kill the tapeworm and its head, which controls the parasite's growth.

Roundworms

Nearly every puppy is born with roundworms, so it is routine to treat for this type of helminth postnatally. Older dogs can also get roundworms, sometimes from ingesting soil contaminated with their eggs. As it develops from egg into adult, the roundworm moves through various body systems, and at different stages can be found in the stomach, intestines, lung, organ or muscle tissue, and even the breast milk of nursing dams.

Signs of infestation include a pot belly, dull coat, failure to thrive, gagging cough, vomiting (often of worms), and even death in young puppies. Worms may also be present in the stool. They are several inches (cm) long and look like pale strands of motile spaghetti.

Hookworms

These small, narrow worms live in the soil and are found in the feces of infected animals. Hookworms fasten to the small intestine of the host dog. Acute infestation may be present in puppies. Symptoms include anemia and bloody diarrhea. In adult dogs or with any long-term infestation, symptoms also include diarrhea and anemia, in addition to weight loss and weakness.

Whipworms

Whipworms are about 2 inches (5.1 cm) long, and as their name implies, resemble a whip. Dogs become infected from soil contaminated with worm eggs. Adult worms fasten to the wall of the large intestine. Signs of infestation include diarrhea, weight loss, and an overall unhealthy appearance. It may be necessary to examine multiple stool samples before the presence of whipworms can be confirmed.

As part of promoting your Pom's good health, internal parasites should be prevented by keeping his outdoor play area clean, and if your veterinarian recommends it, by placing him on a preventative.

If your dog acquires worms, he should receive treatment to kill the parasite. Be cautious of your own health, as some worms can be transmitted to humans. Take a sample of your dog's stool to the veterinarian for analysis and to receive the correct deworming meds, if he has symptoms that indicate a possible worm infestation. At his annual well-dog exam, you can provide a stool sample, which is a good way to stay ahead of internal parasite problems.

Puppies are routinely born with roundworms, a condition that's quickly and easily treated.

HOLISTIC AND ALTERNATIVE HEALTHCARE

Like human medicine, veterinary medicine has kept pace with technology. More high-tech diagnostic testing and treatments are available for dogs each year. But like human medicine, veterinary medicine also has areas where technological advancement has not been able to increase cure rates or promote a better quality of health, usually in chronic conditions where symptoms tend to linger throughout a dog's lifetime.

As a result, some owners have turned to alternative treatment methods that might improve their dog's quality of life in such chronic disease states. These new options incorporate a variety of ancient and new approaches to treatment. Holistic healthcare focuses on treating the whole dog, not just the illness or injury, while at the same time reducing the discomfort and stress of treatment. This practice emphasizes balance and encompasses a combination of traditional and alternative medicines. Holistic practitioners view the canine patient with compassion and respect, and try to choose less invasive techniques which maximize effectiveness and minimize harm to the dog.

"A truly holistic view involves looking at all options and choosing what works best with the fewest side effects," describes veterinary practitioner Shawn Messonnier, DVM, author of *The Natural Health Bible for Dogs & Cats*, and columnist of *The Holistic Pet*. "I'm a conventional doctor by training, and I use conventional therapies in my practice. Whenever possible, I like to integrate as many different therapies as possible, since the best results in my practice tend to occur when conventional therapies are combined with complementary therapies. The holistic approach looks at all treatment options and chooses what works best for each patient."

Therapies—or complementary modalities—can include chiropractic, acupuncture, homeopathy, herbal medicine, acupressure, massage, magnetic therapy, flower essences, crystals, energy healing, and special diets and nutritional supplements.

Acupuncture

The philosophy on which acupuncture is based purports that disease is created when an imbalance of energy occurs in the body. Treatment consists of gently inserting very fine needles at specific locations, believed to be energy points and lines, in the body to redirect and rebalance the energy. Stimulation of these points results in actual physiological and biochemical changes that produce a healing effect.

Acupuncture treatment may produce mild discomfort but is well tolerated by most dogs.

This method has been used on animals for at least 4,000 years to help relieve pain and treat musculoskeletal disorders, nervous disorders, and diseases of the urinary tract, gastrointestinal tract, respiratory system and the skin.

Acupressure

Acupressure is similar to acupuncture in its philosophy and the use of specific points during treatment, except that no needles are used. Conditions treated are similar, but effects of the treatment may not be as profound

For the overall care and well-being of your Pomeranian, you may want to consider some alternative health treatments.

as in acupuncture. Many acupuncturists are also qualified to do acupressure, and some trained pet massage therapists can provide this treatment as well.

Massage

Massage has become a popular and effective way to assist healing of some injuries and certain disorders of the musculoskeletal system. Massage for dogs reduces stress and relieves pain. If you think your Pom might benefit from massage, ask your veterinarian for a referral to a therapist. Books on pet massage are also available to help you learn several techniques for use on your dog at home.

AAVA

For assistance in locating a certified veterinary acupuncturist, contact the American Academy of Veterinary Acupuncture (AAVA), www.aava.org.

Chiropractic

For decades, humans have opted to receive chiropractic treatment, the gentle manipulation of the spine and skeletal system. Trained veterinary chiropractors are now accessible to dogs. This form of treatment operates on the theory that in order to function properly, the body needs to be in correct alignment.

Accidents, stress which causes muscles to tense, abrupt movements, athletic activity, injuries, and more can result in subtle shifts in placement of the joints or spine, and resulting misalignment of the skeletal structure. Chiropractic believes that this causes simultaneous disruption of signals from the nervous system to affected areas, which increases pain and slows healing. The body is returned to proper alignment through adjustment, a treatment which does not produce discomfort. Veterinary chiropractors can be located through the American Veterinary Chiropractic Association (AVCA), www.animalchiropractic.org.

Homeopathy, Flower Essences

In traditional treatment, medicines are considered weapons in a battle against illness and are used to fight symptoms. The principle in homeopathy is nearly opposite: like cures like, by activating the body's natural resources to gently heal itself. Homeopathy uses "remedies" that in healthy individuals would cause the same symptoms of disease that the sick exhibit. This practice isn't just a wild theory; its founder, Dr. Samuel Hahnemann, developed the system in the 1800s after extensive scientific research.

Remedies, which capture the "energetic essence" of the disease state they are used to cure, are derived from plant, mineral, animal, bacterial, viral, or other naturally occurring sources. Flower essences, originally created by a homeopathic practitioner, are mild remedies made from flowering plants and believed to work on the mind or emotions. Homeopathic veterinarians can be found through the Academy of Veterinary Homeopathy (AVH), www.theavh.org.

Herbal or Botanical Medicine

Throughout the millennia, as long as people have been getting sick, there have been healers and practitioners who used herbs to treat disease. Because dogs manifest disease in a manner similar to humans, herbs used to treat people may also be used to medicate dogs.

Herbal preparations are made from different parts of a plant—roots, leaves, or buds—and are biochemically active. Because of these chemical properties, herbs can be used like drugs to treat various conditions. Traditional prescription drugs today are still sometimes manufactured from plant products. But just like drugs, they can have side effects or interact with other medications or herbs.

Herbs tend to be useful in chronic conditions. However, keep in mind that herbs generally take longer to be effective, and may produce milder results. If you want to see if herbal treatment might be helpful for your Pom, consult a veterinarian who is experienced in this practice. A partial listing is available from the Veterinary Botanical Medicine Association (VBMA) www.vbma.org.

FIRST AID AND EMERGENCY CARE

Would you know what to do if your dog had an accident or became critically ill during the hours when your veterinarian's office is closed? If you live in an urban, or even a progressive but semi-rural area, it's likely that there is a veterinary emergency clinic where you can take your Pom. Regardless, you still need to recognize when your dog requires emergency care and be able to provide first aid until you can get him to a veterinarian. Following are descriptions of symptoms of critical conditions and some first-aid techniques to use at home or in transit to a clinic.

Nutrition and Nutritional Supplements

The treatment of many diseases often starts with a special diet, such as the reduction of sugars and carbohydrates in diabetes. Condition-specific foods should not only be convenient for an owner to provide, but also appeal to the dog, as well as be free of possibly harmful additives like artificial colors or preservatives.

Nutritional supplements, such as vitamins, minerals, amino acids, fatty acids, and other key nutrients, can be given to support specific organs, tissues or body systems. This may be done following recovery from an illness in order to maintain health and reduce the likelihood of the problem recurring. Before putting your dog on a special diet or supplements, consult with your veterinarian or a veterinary nutritionist.

"Because there are a number of possible treatments, any disease a Pomeranian might acquire could be treated with a variety of therapies," Dr. Messonnier says, "For example, in some diseases, such as hepatic microvascular dysplasia (a liver defect where ducts are not properly placed), there really aren't any conventional therapies. But this disease responds very well to a combination of diet, nutritional supplements, herbs, and homeopathics."

To ascertain if any alternative, complementary therapies might be helpful in treating your Pom, schedule an appointment with a holistic veterinarian.

Difficulty Breathing or Cardiovascular Distress

Gasping, choking, straining to breathe, noise when breathing, rapid or shallow breathing, extreme anxiety, and collapse. Like human first aid, remember "ABC"—check airway, breathing and circulation. Chest compressions or artificial respiration may be needed.

1. Open dog's mouth, clear saliva and remove any foreign objects if possible.
2. Lay dog on right side and place both hands on chest; press down with sharp motion and quickly release. If dog doesn't begin breathing, start artificial respiration.
3. Pull tongue forward, then hold mouth tightly closed with hand.
4. Put mouth over nose, covering nostrils, and blow gently for two to three seconds. The chest should expand if airway is unobstructed.
5. Continue respirations until dog begins to breath on own.
6. If loss of respiration is due to drowning, hold dog upside down so water runs out of the mouth. Head should be positioned lower than body.
7. If heart is not beating, or no pulse can be felt, heart massage may be necessary. Dog should be in same position as for compressions and have airway cleared.
8. Put thumb on one side and two fingers on other side of breastbone, behind the elbows.
9. Compress (with the positioned thumb and fingers) six times, wait five seconds and repeat. Repetitions may be continued until dog breathes or until no heartbeat is detected for five minutes.

Uncontrolled Bleeding

Copious flow of blood; arterial blood is bright and spurts, blood from veins is dark and flows.

1. Use sterile gauze (or clean cotton cloths if gauze unavailable), place over wound and apply pressure.
2. Tape in place for transport to emergency clinic.
3. Watch for swelling in leg below bandage; slightly loosen bandage to relieve.
4. More severe bleeding may require application of a tourniquet. Wrap several layers of gauze or cloth around wound.
5. Loop gauze tightly, insert stick into top of loop and twist.
6. Loosen stick for five to 10 seconds every 10 to 15 minutes.

VBMA

If you are interested in finding a vet experienced with herbs, a partial listing is available from the Veterinary Botanical Medicine Association (VBMA) www.vbma.org

In an emergency you want to get your Pom to the veterinarian as soon as possible, but knowing how to stabilize your dog before you go is also important.

Distended Abdomen; Acute Abdomen

Bloating with lack of gastrointestinal activity. Or, sudden abdominal pain with retching and vomiting, restlessness, assumption of position with chest down and abdomen up. Possible causes are intestinal obstruction, pancreatitis, urinary stones, ruptured bladder, bloat, or torsion.

Rush to clinic, as all conditions are life-threatening.

• Bloody or violent vomiting or diarrhea also requires immediate treatment.

Inability to Urinate

Straining to urinate, no urine produced, or small amounts of bloody urine.

• Seek immediate treatment; dog may need catheterization. Failure to pass urine can lead to kidney failure and death.

Neurological Symptoms

Staggering gait, tremors, convulsions or seizures, loss of balance, loss of consciousness, sudden loss of vision, tilted head sometimes with circling.

• Keep dog calm and warm.
• Wrap in blanket to prevent self-injury. Get medical attention.

Poison

Many chemicals and plants cause violent illness or death. Symptoms vary with substance ingested but include vomiting, diarrhea, panting, drooling, salivating, difficulty breathing, seizures, loss of bladder or bowel control, coma, and death.

• Immediately try to locate plant or chemical ingested.
• Do not induce vomiting unless certain that it is appropriate; some agents are treated without inducing vomiting, but are diluted with milk instead. Do not induce vomiting if dog is unconscious or having seizures.
• Check on label or with pet poison assistance centers at the ASPCA Animal Poison Control Center, 1-888-4-ANI-HELP or 1-888-426-4435, or National Animal Poison Control Center 1-900-680-0000 or 1-800-548-2423.

- If induction of vomiting is advised, give one teaspoon hydrogen peroxide per five pounds (2.25 kilograms) of weight, to a maximum of three tablespoons. Activated charcoal may also be given, if advised, to help absorb poison.
- As soon as you have done as instructed, seek emergency treatment; poisons can have long-term effects.

Broken Bones; Spinal Injury

- Stabilize break to restrain movement. Avoid moving broken leg or back to limit damage.
- Temporarily splint limb by wrapping loosely in multiple layers of gauze or newspaper.
- Carefully slide onto wood plank or heavy cardboard, or wrap in heavy coat and transport to clinic for treatment. Dog may need to be muzzled, if muzzle doesn't interfere with breathing

Eye Injury

- Flush with sterile saline, cover with sterile pad if drainage or bleeding is moderate to profuse, and get dog to clinic.

Heatstroke; Hypothermia

Exposure to hot weather temperatures can cause fatal heatstroke. Signs are raspy, intensely rapid breathing, very red gums and tongue, thick saliva, moderate to severely elevated body temperature, and vomiting. Progression to death is rapid.

- Move to cool room or area, immerse in cool water, or spray with garden hose. If collapse is imminent, give cool water enema.
- Veterinary treatment may include drugs to reduce heat-related inflammation. Heatstroke is preventable; avoid situations where dog could get overly warm. For example, it only takes a few minutes for an unventilated vehicle, even parked in the shade, to exceed temperatures compatible with life during warm weather.
- Exposure to cold temperatures for prolonged periods can result in hypothermia—loss of minimum body temperature necessary to maintain life. Toy-sized dogs are most susceptible. Signs are violent shivering, apathy and lethargy, body temperature below 97° F (36°C).
- Move to warm room or area. Wrap in towels or blankets.
- Hot water bottles, or heating pads set to "low" can be applied over the towels. Hair dryers on "warm" setting may also help. Dogs

Burns

Uncommon in dogs. Rinse with cool water. Apply antibiotic burn ointment. For severe or chemical burns, seek immediate treatment.

Disasters can strike with little or no warning. Be prepared to save your beloved companion along with the rest of your family. Keep a doggy bag handy, packed with the same supplies you would take if you were traveling with your Pom—food, medicine, papers, and so forth. Have an evacuation plan ready so you know where to go for shelter that will allow your dog to be with you, or have other safe kenneling facilities nearby.

must be monitored during use.

• When dog is warm, give food to return blood sugar (glucose) to normal levels.

Allergic Reactions

Can cause anaphylactic shock, a possibly fatal collapse of the body's systems. Reactions to drugs, insect bites, and some foods can result in hives, vomiting, difficulty breathing, swelling of airways, shock, and death.

• Give antihistamine based on the dosage chart on the packaging for your dog's weight to conscious dogs and rush to emergency clinic.

Accident or Trauma

Due to fall, struck by vehicle, penetrating wound, chest or abdominal wound, broken bones, severe bleeding, or a neck, head or back injury.

• Shock may ensue. Muzzle (unless breathing is impaired), give first aid (ABC), and go for immediate treatment. If muzzle is not available, gauze or strips of any soft cloth such as cotton rags, or even a loose, cloth-covered elastic hair scrunchie may be substituted.

Shock

Possible result of severe, acute trauma, allergy, or illness. Detected by pale gums, shallow respiration, rapid heart rate, weakness or collapse, depression, confusion, and faint pulse.

• Check airway and breathing, treat as described above, control bleeding if applicable.

• Calm dog and keep him warm. Do not impede breathing with muzzle. Rush to emergency clinic.

Skunked!

If your Pom camps with you, or likes to investigate the wildlife in your backyard, at some point he may have an encounter of the stinky kind with a skunk. While skunk spray may cause some burning and watering of his eyes, getting "skunked" is not a medical emergency, but you will need to handle this smelly situation immediately.

Either call your groomer or vet and take your Pom for a deskunking bath (transport him wrapped in a towel and placed in his crate to prevent contaminating your vehicle). Or you can wash out the odor at home. Two formulas you can mix yourself include

readily available ingredients.

1 quart of 3% hydrogen peroxide

1/4 cup of baking soda

1 teaspoon of liquid soap

or

1 pint hydrogen peroxide

2/3 cup baking soda

1 tablespoon liquid soap, preferably citrus based

Mix these when needed; do not store, or else they won't work. Wash, rinse, and repeat if needed. Rinse thoroughly. Condition and dry your Pom's coat as you normally would after any other bath. (See Chapter 5.)

THE SENIOR POMERANIAN

As your Pom ages, there will be changes in his health, such as difficulty moving, seeing, hearing, or chewing. When a dog is a cute puppy bouncing around, it's hard to imagine that he will one day grow old. But aging is inevitable. Providing extra care and support can allow your elderly Pomeranian to live his last days in greater comfort.

Physically, it's important to monitor your dog's weight and nutrition. Health conditions common to older dogs can be worsened by obesity. Foods designed for senior dogs provide essential nutrients in balanced amounts but with fewer calories, reducing the chance of excess weight gain. Older dogs can also become too thin and may require a more appealing food that is higher in calories to maintain proper weight and energy level.

Skin and coat problems that may increase with age can be improved by regular grooming.

Although you may need to change techniques or shorten grooming sessions, don't stop grooming your Pom. Continue to bathe and brush him to keep his fur clean and free of mats. And don't forget to brush his teeth, as always. Bacteria from gum disease can put extra strain on aging organs.

Make sure your older Pom's space is comfortable and safe. Use soft, supportive bedding in a room that isn't too cold, drafty, or damp. Place multiple water bowls throughout the house so he doesn't have to walk too far to get a drink. However, don't stop

First-Aid Kit and Supplies

- Gauze pads, rolled gauze, first-aid tape, rolled cotton, cotton balls, anti-bacterial wipes, self-clinging bandage or vet wrap.
- Rubbing alcohol, hydrogen peroxide, antibiotic ointment, petroleum jelly, sterile saline.
- PeptoBismol or kaopectate (NOTE: ingredients now contain salicylates, an aspirin-like substance that can exacerbate bleeding problems, gastro-intestinal inflammation, or to which some dogs may be sensitive. It may also cause an adverse effect if given with certain other medications), milk of magnesia, Benadryl, Rescue Remedy, activated charcoal capsules.
- Scissors, tweezers, bulb syringe for administering medications, rectal thermometer.
- Paper towels, towel, blanket, zipper-close plastic baggies, hot-cold pack, muzzle.

exercising your dog just because he's getting older—physical activity promotes better circulation and digestion, which tend to be problematic in older dogs. Plan exercise around your Pom's limitations, and don't let him overdo it.

As he ages, take your senior Pom to the vet about every six months for a wellness and preventive exam. This provides an opportunity to catch age-related problems as they occur.

Aging also affects emotional health. Changes in the brain may be observed in altered sleep-wake patterns, moments of disorientation, or changes in behavior. Canine nutritionists have discovered that antioxidants in the diet can be beneficial for the senior dog's mental health. It has also been shown that keeping your older Pom's mind stimulated helps. Providing new toys, playing games that make him think, and continued interaction with people and pet friends are all ways to help him stay alert.

But probably the most important part of keeping the older Pomeranian healthy is to make him happy and to love him as much in his old age as you did when he was a puppy. Tips on how to care for an older dog can be found on the web at www.srdogs.com .

SAYING GOODBYE

An old cliché says that all good things must come to an end. Sadly, this is true even for the life of a beloved dog. No matter when it occurs for your dog—at the end of a long life or following an early death from accident or disease—it will be too soon. And it will be one of the most sorrowful events in your life.

At that time, you may be called upon to make what may be the most difficult decision you ever face: whether or not to euthanize your best friend. Euthanization is done as humanely as possible by giving an overdose injection of a strong sedative. If your dog is anxious, a mild tranquilizer may be given prior to help calm him. Most dogs simply lie down and close their eyes. A few may vocalize or experience mild twitching, but for the most part, their passing appears peaceful. It is heart-wrenching to decide to end your dog's life, but it is equally painful to watch him lose his dignity or die suffering or in pain.

If you never had to euthanize a pet, it may be difficult to believe, but it is likely that your dog will let you know when he is ready to go. It may even be clear to you that he is asking you to help him be released. Or your Pomeranian may pass quietly in his sleep.

Whichever way your dog's death occurs, you may experience doubts about your actions and choices. You will also grieve and be intensely sad over your loss. These feelings are normal, but you don't have to suffer in silence. Nearly all veterinary colleges offer toll-free telephone numbers for bereaved owners to call and speak with a trained grief counselor. For more information visit www.petloss.com or www.rainbowsbridge.com.

Your days spent in each other's company will be over, but you will be left with your memories. The best way to prepare for the eventual loss of your Pomeranian is to make the most of your time together now. Live your life with your canine companion in such a way that you have few regrets. Treat him well, take good care of him, play with him, travel with him, and love him. Then when the day arrives that you say your final goodbyes, your memories will be that much sweeter, as the bond you once shared lives on in your heart.

Your special friend is one who you will remember forever.

AKC POMERANIAN BREED STANDARD

General Appearance: The Pomeranian is a compact, short-backed, active toy dog. He has a soft, dense undercoat with a profuse harsh-textured outer coat. His heavily plumed tail is set high and lies flat on his back. He is alert in character, exhibits intelligence in expression, is buoyant in deportment, and is inquisitive by nature. The Pomeranian is cocky, commanding, and animated as he gaits. He is sound in composition and action.

Size, Proportion and Substance: The average weight of the Pomeranian is from 3 to 7 pounds, with the ideal weight for the show specimen being 4 to 6 pounds. Any dog over or under the limits is objectionable. However, overall quality is to be favored over size. The distance from the point of shoulder to the point of buttocks is slightly shorter than from the highest point of the withers to the ground. the distance from the brisket to the ground is half the height at the withers. He is medium-boned, and the length of his legs is in proportion to a well-balanced frame. When examined, he feels sturdy.

Head: The head is in balance with the body. The muzzle is rather short, straight, fine, free of lippiness and never snipey. His expression is alert and may be referred to as fox-like. The skull is closed. The top of the skull is slightly rounded, but not domed. When viewed from the front and side, one sees small ears which are mounted high and carried erect. To form a wedge, visualize a line from the tip of the nose ascending through the center of the eyes and the tip of the ears. The eyes are dark, bright, medium in size and almond-shaped. They are set well into the skull on either side of a well-pronounced stop. The pigmentation is black on the nose and eye rims except self-colored in brown, beaver, and blue dogs. The teeth meet in a scissors bite. One tooth out of alignment is acceptable. Major Faults: Round, domed skull; under-shot mouth; overshot mouth.

Neck, Topline, Body: The neck is short with its base set well into the shoulders to allow the head to be carried high. The back is short with a level topline. The body is compact and well-ribbed with brisket reaching the elbow. The plumed tail is one of the characteristics of the breed, and lies flat and straight on the back.

Forequarters: The Pomeranian has sufficient layback of shoulders to carry the neck and head proud and high. The shoulders and legs are moderately muscled. The length of the shoulder blade and upper arm are equal. The forelegs are straight and parallel to each other. Height from elbows to withers approximately equals height from ground to elbow. The pasterns are straight and strong. The feet are well-arched, compact, and turn neither in nor out. He stands well up on his toes. Dewclaws may be removed. Major Faults: Down in pasterns.

Hindquarters: The angulation of the hindquarters balances that of the forequarters. The buttocks are well behind the set of the tail. The thighs are moderately muscled with stifles that are moderately bent and clearly defined. The hocks are perpendicular to the ground and the legs are straight and parallel to each other. The feet are well-arched, compact, and turn neither in nor out. He stands well up on his toes. Dewclaws, if any on the hind legs may be removed. Major Faults: Cowhocks or lack of soundness in hind legs or stifles.

Gait: The Pomeranian's gait is smooth, free, balanced and vigorous. He has good reach in his forequarters and strong drive with his hindquarters. Each rear leg moves in line with the foreleg on the same side. To achieve balance, his legs converge slightly inward toward a center line beneath his body. The rear and front legs are thrown neither in nor out. The topline remains level, and his overall balance and outline are maintained.

Coat: A Pomeranian is noted for its double coat. The undercoat is soft and dense. The outer-coat is long, straight, glistening and harsh in texture. A thick undercoat will hold up and permit the guard hair to stand off from the Pomeranian's body. The coat is abundant from the neck and fore part of shoulders and chest, forming a frill which extends over the shoulders and chest. The head and leg coat is tightly packed and shorter in length than that of the body. The forequarters are well-feathered to the hock. The tail is profusely covered with long, harsh, spreading straight hair. Trimming for neatness and a clean outline is permissible. Major Faults: Soft, flat or open coat.

Color: All colors, patterns, and variations there-of are allowed and must be judged on an equal basis. Patterns: Black and Tan - tan or rust sharply defined, appearing above each eye and on muzzle, throat, and forechest, on all legs and feet and below the tail. The richer the tan the more desirable; Brindle - the base color is gold, red, or orange-brindled with strong black cross stripes; Parti-color - is white with any other color distributed in patches with a white blaze preferred on the head. Classifications: The Open Classes at specialty shows may be divided by color as follows: Open Red, Orange, Cream, and Sable; Open Black, Brown, and Blue; Open Any Other Color, Pattern, or Variation.

Temperament: The Pomeranian is an extrovert, exhibiting great intelligence and a vivacious spirit, making him a great companion dog as well as a competitive show dog.

Even though a Toy dog, the Pomeranian must be subject to the same requirements of soundness and structure prescribed for all breeds, and any deviation from the ideal described in the standard should be penalized to the extent of the deviation.

Approved December 9, 1996
Effective January 31, 1997

KENNEL CLUB BREED STANDARD

General Appearance: Compact, short-coupled dog, well knit in frame. Exhibiting great intelligence in expression; activity and buoyancy in deportment.

Characteristics: Sound, vivacious and dainty.

Temperament: Extrovert, lively and intelligent.

Head and Skull: Head and nose foxy in outline, skull slightly flat, large in proportion to muzzle which finishes finely and free from lippiness. Nose black in white, orange and shaded sable dogs; brown in chocolate-tipped sable dogs, but in other colours may be self-coloured, never parti-coloured or flesh.

Eyes: Medium size, slightly oval, not full, or set too wide apart; bright, dark and showing great intelligence. In white, orange, shaded sable and cream dogs, rims black.

Ears: Small, not set too wide apart, nor too low down, but carried perfectly erect.

Mouth: Jaws strong, with a perfect, regular and complete scissor bite, i.e. upper teeth closely overlapping lower teeth and set square to the jaws.

Neck: Rather short and well set into shoulders.

Forequarters: Shoulders clean and well laid back. Fine-boned legs, perfectly straight, of medium length in due proportion to size of dog.

Body: Back short, body compact, well ribbed up, barrel well rounded. Chest fairly deep, not too wide but in proportion to size of dog.

Hindquarters: Fine-boned, legs neither cow-hocked nor wide behind; medium angulation.

Feet: Small, compact and cat-like.

Tail: Characteristic of breed, high set, turned over back and carried flat and straight, profusely covered with long, harsh, spreading hair.

Gait/Movement: Free moving, brisk and buoyant.

Coat: Two coats, an undercoat and an outer coat. Former soft, fluffy; the latter long, perfectly straight, harsh in texture and covering whole of body; very abundant round neck and fore part of shoulders and chest; forming frill, extending over shoulders. Forequarters well feathered, thighs and hindlegs well feathered to hocks.

Colour: All colours permissible, but free from black or white shadings. Whole colours are: white, black, brown, light or dark, blue as pale as possible. Orange which should be self-coloured and bright as possible. Beaver. Cream dogs have black noses and black eye rims. Whites must be quite free from lemon or any other colour. A few white hairs, in any of the self-coloured dogs permissible but undesirable. Dogs (other than white) with white or tan markings highly undesirable and not considered whole coloured specimens. In parti-coloured dogs, colours evenly distributed on body in patches; a dog with white or tan feet or chest not a parti-coloured dog. Shaded sables should be shaded throughout with three or more colours, the hair to be as uniformly shaded as possible, and with no patches of self-colour. In mixed classes, where whole coloured and parti-coloured Pomeranians compete together, the preference should, if in all other points they are equal, be given to the whole coloured specimens.

Size: Ideal weight: dogs: 1.8-2 kgs (4-41/2 lbs); bitches: 2-2.5 kgs (41/2-51/2 lbs).

Faults: Any departure from the foregoing points should be considered a fault and the seriousness with which the fault should be regarded should be in exact proportion to its degree and its effect upon the health and welfare of the dog.

Note: Male animals should have two apparently normal testicles fully descended into the scrotum.

March 1994

WHAT TO DO WHEN IT DOESN'T WORK OUT

If you've done your homework, chosen the perfect breed and the right Pomeranian for your home, then chances are good that you and your dog will live happily ever after. But what can be done if the relationship with your dog isn't as happy as a fairy tale? First, realize that not every day with a dog is a good one. Try to learn to accept the bad along with the good. However, if you and the dog are continually unhappy despite your best efforts, the relationship may not be working out for either of you. Before you give up:

- Have your dog thoroughly examined by a veterinarian. Some behavior problems are caused by medical issues, many of which can be treated;
- Consult with a behaviorist or training consultant who may be able to correct problematic behavior;
- Enter and complete a training class with your Pom;
- Examine your lifestyle—can it be changed to adapt to your dog's needs? Can your dog's exercise or nutrition be changed to help cope with a problem?

If these steps don't resolve the problem, some signs that may indicate your dog might be better off in a different home include:

- A drastic change in your life that has rendered you incapable of caring for your dog on a long-term basis, either financially, physically or emotionally;
- An inability to provide needed medical care on a regular basis;
- A lack of time or finances to groom your Pom and his coat is matted most of the time;
- Your dog is often alone or is crated or confined most of the time, is depressed and losing interest in his surroundings;
- You become uninterested in your dog or his welfare;
- You are emotionally unable to cope with your dog's problems and have relegated him to the yard or basement, or you have resorted to using physical punishment on your dog.

If it becomes necessary to rehome your dog:

- Contact your breeder first about taking the dog back;
- Locate the closest Pomeranian rescue group and ask them to foster your dog for eventual placement into a new home;
- Provide the rescue group with a thorough and honest history of your dog's health and behavior, which gives him the best chance of getting a good – permanent – home.
- Do not sell or give your dog away to strangers that may not be qualified to care for him.
- Don't turn your dog into a "kill-shelter" unless you have exhausted all other options or have an extreme emergency. If you must take your dog to a shelter, immediately notify a Pom rescue group so that he can be removed and placed in a foster home.
- Do not, under any circumstances, leave your dog behind when you move, or drive him away from home and turn him loose...or worse! Shelters, rescue groups, and even veterinarians are available and willing to help.

For assistance in locating a rescue group or shelter, see the References section.

APPENDIX B

ASSOCIATIONS AND ORGANIZATIONS

Breed Clubs

American Kennel Club (AKC)
5580 Centerview Drive
Raleigh, NC 27606
Telephone: (919) 233-9767
Fax: (919) 233-3627
E-mail: info@akc.org
www.akc.org

American Pomeranian Club
Corresponding Secretary:
Cindy Boulware
6450 Rolling Heights Cir.
Kaufman, TX 75142
Email: contact@
AmericanPomeranianClub.
org
www.americanpomeranian
club.org

Canadian Kennel Club (CKC)
89 Skyway Avenue, Suite 100
Etobicoke, Ontario M9W 6R4
Telephone: (416) 675-5511
Fax: (416) 675-6506
E-mail: information@ckc.ca
www.ckc.ca

Federation Cynologique Internationale (FCI)
Secretariat General de la FCI
Place Albert 1er, 13
B – 6530 Thuin
Belqique
www.fci.be

The Kennel Club
1 Clarges Street
London
W1J 8AB
Telephone: 0870 606 6750
Fax: 0207 518 1058
www.the-kennel-club.org.uk

Pomeranian Club of Canada
Secretary: Paddy Bruce
#2 - 69 Charlotte Drive
Charlottetown, PEI
C1A 2N8
Telephone: (902) 628-6680
Email: paddybruce@
islandtelecom.com
www.pcoc.net

Pomeranian Club (United Kingdom)
Secretary: Mrs. A.Cawthera
Wheatley Grange,
Wheatleasowes
Nr Telford, TF6 6DS
Telephone: 01952 204298

United Kennel Club (UKC)
100 E. Kilgore Road
Kalamazoo, MI 49002-5584
Telephone: (269) 343-9020
Fax: (269) 343-7037
E-mail: pbickell@ukcdogs.com
www.ukcdogs.com

Pet Sitters

National Association of Professional Pet Sitters
15000 Commerce Parkway,
Suite C
Mt. Laurel, New Jersey 08054
Telephone: (856) 439-0324
Fax: (856) 439-0525
E-mail: napps@ahint.com
www.petsitters.org

Pet Sitters International
201 East King Street
King, NC 27021-9161
Telephone: (336) 983-9222
Fax: (336) 983-5266
E-mail: info@petsit.com
www.petsit.com

Rescue Organizations and Animal Welfare Groups

American Humane Association (AHA)
63 Inverness Drive East
Englewood, CO 80112
Telephone: (303) 792-9900
Fax: 792-5333
www.americanhumane.org

American Society for the Prevention of Cruelty to Animals (ASPCA)
424 E. 92nd Street
New York, NY 10128-6804
Telephone: (212) 876-7700
www.aspca.org

Pomeranian Club of Canada
Rescue Coordinator,
Christine Surtees
151 Greystone Crescent,
R.R. #4
Almonte, ON, K0A 1A0,
Canada
Telephone: (613) 256-2019
E-mail: pomkees@comnet.ca
www.pcoc.net/rescue.htm

Royal Society for the Prevention of Cruelty to Animals (RSPCA)
Telephone: 0870 3335 999
Fax: 0870 7530 284
www.rspca.org.uk

The Humane Society of the United States (HSUS)
2100 L Street, NW
Washington DC 20037
Telephone: (202) 452-1100
www.hsus.org
Breed Rescue

Sports

Canine Freestyle
Federation, Inc.
Secretary: Brandy Clymire
E-Mail: secretary@canine-freestyle.org
www.caninefreestyle.org

International Agility Link (IAL)
Global Administrator:
Steve Drinkwater
E-mail: yunde@powerup.au
www.agilityclick.com/~ial

North American Dog Agility Council
11522 South Hwy 3
Cataldo, ID 83810
ww.nadac.com

North American Flyball Association
www.flyball.org
1400 West Devon Avenue #512
Chicago, IL 6066
800-318-6312

United States Dog Agility Association
P.O. Box 850955
Richardson, TX 75085-0955
Telephone: (972) 487-2200
www.usdaa.com

World Canine Freestyle Organization
P.O. Box 350122
Brooklyn, NY 11235-2525
Telephone: (718) 332-8336
www.worldcaninefreestyle.org

Therapy

Delta Society
875 124th Ave NE, Suite 101
Bellevue, WA 98005
Telephone: (425) 226-7357
Fax: (425) 235-1076
E-mail: info@deltasociety.org
wwww.deltasociety.org

Therapy Dogs Incorporated
PO Box 5868
Cheyenne, WY 82003
Telephone: (877) 843-7364
E-mail: therdog@sisna.com
www.therapydogs.com

Therapy Dogs International (TDI)
88 Bartley Road
Flanders, NJ 07836
Telephone: (973) 252-9800
Fax: (973) 252-7171
E-mail: tdi@gti.net
www.tdi-dog.org

Training

Association of Pet Dog Trainers (APDT)
150 Executive Center Drive
Box 35
Greenville, SC 29615
Telephone: (800) PET-DOGS
Fax: (864) 331-0767
E-mail: information@apdt.com
www.apdt.com

National Association of Dog Obedience Instructors
PMB 369
729 Grapevine Hwy.
Hurst, TX 76054-2085
www.nadoi.org

Veterinary and Health Resources

Academy of Veterinary Homeopathy (AVH)
P.O. Box 9280
Wilmington, DE 19809
Telephone: (866) 652-1590
Fax: (866) 652-1590
E-mail: office@TheAVH.org
www.theavh.org

American Academy of Veterinary Acupuncture (AAVA)
100 Roscommon Drive, Suite 320
Middletown, CT 06457
Telephone: (860) 635-6300
Fax: (860) 635-6400
E-mail: office@aava.org
www.aava.org

American Animal Hospital Association (AAHA)
P.O. Box 150899
Denver, CO 80215-0899
Telephone: (303) 986-2800
Fax: (303) 986-1700
E-mail: info@aahanet.org
www.aahanet.org/index.cfm

American College of Veterinary Internal Medicine (ACVIM)
1997 Wadsworth Blvd., Suite A
Lakewood, CO 80214-5293
Telephone: (800) 245-9081
Fax: (303) 231-0880
Email: ACVIM@ACVIM.org
www.acvim.org

American College of Veterinary Ophthalmologists (ACVO)
P.O. Box 1311
Meridian, Idaho 83860
Telephone: (208) 466-7624
Fax: (208) 466-7693
E-mail: office@acvo.com
www.acvo.com

American Holistic Veterinary Medical Association (AHVMA)
2218 Old Emmorton Road
Bel Air, MD 21015
Telephone: (410) 569-0795
Fax: (410) 569-2346
E-mail: office@ahvma.org
www.ahvma.org

American Veterinary Medical Association (AVMA)
1931 North Meacham Road – Suite 100
Schaumburg, IL 60173
Telephone: (847) 925-8070
Fax: (847) 925-1329
E-mail: avmainfo@avma.org
www.avma.org

ASPCA Animal Poison Control Center
1717 South Philo Road, Suite 36
Urbana, IL 61802
Telephone: (888) 426-4435
www.aspca.org

British Veterinary Association (BVA)
7 Mansfield Street
London
W1G 9NQ
Telephone: 020 7636 6541
Fax: 020 7436 2970
E-mail: bvahq@bva.co.uk
www.bva.co.uk

Canine Eye Registration Foundation (CERF)
VMDB/CERF
1248 Lynn Hall
625 Harrison St.
Purdue University
West Lafayette, IN 47907-2026
Telephone: (765) 494-8179
E-mail: CERF@vmbd.org
www.vmdborg

Orthopedic Foundation for Animals (OFA)
2300 NE Nifong Blvd
Columbus, Missouri 65201-3856
Telephone: (573) 442-0418
Fax: (573) 875-5073
Email: ofa@offa.org
www.offa.org

Severe Hair Loss Syndrome study
Liz Hansen
University of Missouri
College of Veterinary Medicine
Columbia, MO 65211
Telephone: (573) 884-3712
E-mail: HansenL@missouri.edu
www.akcchf.org

PUBLICATIONS

Magazines

AKC *Family Dog*
American Kennel Club
260 Madison Avenue
New York, NY 10016
Telephone: (800) 490-5675
E-mail: familydog@akc.org
www.akc.org/pubs/familydog

AKC *Gazette*
American Kennel Club
260 Madison Avenue
New York, NY 10016
Telephone: (800) 533-7323
E-mail: gazette@akc.org
www.akc.org/pubs/gazette

Dog & Kennel
Pet Publishing, Inc.
7-L Dundas Circle
Greensboro, NC 27407
Telephone: (336) 292-4272
Fax: (336) 292-4272
E-mail: info@petpublishing.com
www.dogandkennel.com

Dog Fancy
Subscription Department
P.O. Box 53264
Boulder, CO 80322-3264
Telephone: (800) 365-4421
E-mail: barkback@dogfancy.com
www.dogfancy.com

Dogs Monthly
Ascot House
High Street, Ascot,
Berkshire SL5 7JG
United Kingdom
Telephone: 0870 730 8433
Fax: 0870 730 8431
E-mail: admin@rtc-associates.freeserve.co.uk
www.corsini.co.uk/dogsmonthly

ACKNOWLEDGEMENTS

Research for this project was a slow process, with information sometimes being slow to come out for a stranger, rather like some Poms I met. All the people with whom I spoke were most willing to provide information and were helpful providing insight into what it's like to live with a Pomeranian. Like their dogs, I found them to be intelligent, busy and energetic, and friendly. To all of you—Pom people and Poms —thank you for your efforts.

For the Pomeranians: May the information in this book help bring about a world where no more Pomeranians ever need rescued.

ABOUT THE AUTHOR

Lexiann Grant is an internationally published, award-winning pet writer and photographer who has raised, trained, shown, written, and spoken about dogs and cats for many years. She is a professional member of the Dog Writers Association of America and has been a recipient of the Maxwell Medallion eight times. Ms. Grant works full-time in her home office, where much of her time is spent observing the pets with whom she lives. In addition to her life that revolves around animals, Ms. Grant cycles, skis, practices yoga, and is a chocolate addict. She and her husband reside in southeastern Ohio with three dogs, four cats, and four bicycles.

PHOTO CREDITS

Larry Allen: 66, 107
Max Blain (Shutterstock): 64, 195
Linda Bucklin (Shutterstock): 141, 171, 174, 180, 186
Lexiann Grant: 175
Patricia Marroquin (Shutterstock): 12
Theresa Martinez (Shutterstock): 142, 149
revelationmedia (Shutterstock): 59
Laurin Rinder (Shutterstock): 70, 192
Candace Schwadron (Shutterstock): 51
April Turner (Shutterstock): 62

Wiz Data, Inc. (Shutterstock): 88
All other photos courtesy of Isabelle Francais and TFH Archives